NO TRUE TRUTH

Darren Pleasance

A HANDBOOK FOR INSPIRED LIVING

True North: A Handbook for Inspired Living

987654321
First Edition
Printed in the United States of America.

Cover design by James Sholly, Pithy Wordsmithery
Interior layout by Jan Zucker, Pithy Wordsmithery
Copy Editing by Nils Kuehn, Pithy Wordsmithery
Proofreading by Scott Morrow, Pithy Wordsmithery

ISBN: 979-8-9893736-0-4 (paperback)
ISBN: 979-8-9893736-1-1 (ebook)
ISBN: 979-8-9893736-2-8 (hardcover)

Darren Pleasance
hello@darrenpleasance.com
www.darrenpleasance.com

Library of Congress Control Number: 2023922460

Praise

"*True North* reminds us that inspiration isn't just about fleeting moments but about aligning our lives with our deepest truths, about finding your deepest purpose. An essential read for anyone looking to transition their life from success to one of significance."

— Peter H. Diamandis, MD;
founder, XPRIZE Foundation; cofounder, Singularity University;
New York Times Best Seller author of Abundance, Bold, and
The Future Is Faster than You Think

"I've experienced some of the most extreme highs and lows that life can dish out. The guidance that Darren provides in *True North* is spot on for anyone looking to build a life that keeps them energized while navigating the inevitable challenges that come our way."

— Drew Bledsoe, former NFL quarterback,
founder/owner of Doubleback Winery

"Defining *True North* is perhaps the most vital work we do in any life arena, as is figuring out how to get there. In this enlightening work and in his inimitable style, Darren Pleasance gives readers the tools and inspiration to begin a personal journey toward joy."

— Maria Martinez,
COO, Cisco

"Living your best life requires a delicate blend of elements, which Darren astutely and accurately presents."

— Deke Sharon,
music director of *Pitch Perfect*,
producer of NBC's *The Sing-Off*

"This is *Think and Grow Rich* meets *The Art of Happiness*. Darren Pleasance shares his wisdom on getting past fear by having the courage and confidence to embrace the unknown so you can pursue what truly matters. His authentic perspective will guide you to shake up your routine, experience financial freedom, and live the life you have always imagined."

— David Rosell, wealth manager,
speaker, author of *Failure Is Not an Option*,
Keep Climbing, and *In the Know*

"Darren has skillfully described techniques you can use to live your life with purpose—an almost sacred obligation we have from receiving this astounding gift of life in our amazing universe. I can personally attest that Darren's methods work. You may never have an opportunity to sit on a launch pad, strapped to a rocket with four-and-a-half million pounds of explosive propellant under your seat. But if you did, you would feel the same sense of calm I did as the countdown clock progressed toward zero. You would be present, experiencing every moment, not worrying about the outcome or result, but processing everything that is happening. Be here, now! Read Darren's book and learn how to live your life with purpose—and have fun on your journey."

— Jim Wetherbee, captain, U.S. Navy (ret.);
former astronaut, NASA; author of *Controlling Risk
in a Dangerous World*

"Darren has turned his hard-earned wisdom and insights into a clear and actionable guide. So much of the book resonated with me and reflected my own observations and experiences. *True North* is a fast and easy read for anyone who is on a journey to live an inspired and purposeful life."

— Selin Song, President,
Google Customer Solutions

"As a person who has always broken my own trails and experienced the immense lack of role models living truly inspiring lives, I've been missing *True North* in my backpack. The book serves as a compass for anyone trying to find their path to a life filled with passion and alignment with one's own authentic definition of success. *True North* is an essential read for anyone looking to lead a life of significance and serves as a map, mentor, and muse all in one."

— Jessica Nordlander, COO,
Thought Exchange; Canada's Top 40 under 40;
Sweden's Most Innovative Leader

"*True North* provides direction, but most importantly, it awakens the innate guide within, lighting up the hearts and minds of those who read it, inspiring a genuine and purpose driven life."

— Jessie Pavelka, NBC's *The Biggest Loser*
TEDx speaker, author

"Whether you're looking to make a career pivot or want to live a more fulfilling life, *True North* is a perfect playbook on how to live YOUR life to the fullest—not someone else's dream for you. It's a perfect guide on how to intentionally create the life you've always dreamed of."

— Stephanie Goetz, former NBC News anchor,
founder Goetz Communications,
TEDx speaker, jet pilot

"*True North* is a must-read for anyone looking to live their passion. Through captivating storytelling of personal experiences in some of the world's largest and most successful enterprises, Darren Pleasance shows us how to find our drum beat and live what we love wherever we are. Truly inspiring!"

— Andy Cunningham, author,
CEO of Cunningham Collective,
Baby Boomer parent

Dedication

This book is dedicated to all those who seek to live life to the fullest, continuously looking forward to the journey ahead while feeling gratitude and fulfillment for the path already traveled.

Table of Contents

Preface

I discovered early in my teenage years that I had a fascination with aviation. It was something I stumbled upon by accident one day when I came across a man at a local park flying a radio-control model airplane with his nephew. That encounter sparked an interest in flying that I didn't even know I had. Over the subsequent years, that interest became a full-blown love affair. It also formed my first view of what I wanted to do when I grew up: I wanted to become an airline pilot, and I was going to do whatever it took to make that happen.

Alas, it never happened. A variety of roadblocks ended up getting in my way over the years, starting with discovering that I suffer from a color-vision deficiency, then finding myself entering a cut-throat job market in which I would have to compete with thousands of pilots who'd lost their jobs at Braniff, Eastern, Pan Am, TWA, and other airlines that went bankrupt during the years I was working to become an airline pilot. But this isn't to say that I never got to become a pilot. I still flew airplanes, early on as a glider tow pilot, then as a flight instructor, then later as an Alaska bush pilot, and eventually as a corporate jet pilot flying for the likes of John Travolta and other high-net-worth individuals.

This life journey was moving along nicely as I headed into my late 20s with my newly refined goal of just being a "pilot" rather than an "airline pilot." But once again, life threw a curveball my way. After the business owner I was flying for suffered a major heart attack and ended up passing away, the company decided that the private jets were no longer required, and I found myself having to decide what to do next. I had learned quite a bit about business by virtue of spending so much time with successful people, so I opted to go to business school. I wasn't necessarily trying to find a career outside aviation, but I figured I could burn a couple years learning something new while I sorted out what my next flying job would be. It was during these two years at the Anderson School of Business at UCLA that I discovered management consulting.

Management consulting is an interesting field in which large, mostly Fortune 500 companies hire these consulting firms to help them with some of the most challenging issues they're trying to resolve. These consultants get to travel the world, stay at nice hotels, eat at nice restaurants, and work with amazing people on interesting topics. Having a strong sense of adventure, I was drawn to the level of variety in what they do.

I started interviewing with these firms as they came through UCLA. But though my classmates would regularly get second interviews and third interviews and finally make it all the way through to attractive job offers, I would never make it past the first round; I pursued dozens of interviews, each one with the same outcome. I can only assume my interviewing skills weren't as polished as those of my classmates—and for sure, my background of flying bush planes in Alaska and then corporate jets for a no-name investment firm in Santa Barbara just didn't stand out as much as the typical, and significantly more respectable, résumés of my classmates.

I did, however, finally end up "getting lucky" (more on this later) when Walter Ulrich, the head of a Boston-based consulting firm, came to UCLA and inquired with the dean: "I have my lunch hour open today; is there anyone in your class of 300 students I should make sure I speak to?" The dean had gotten to know and like me that summer and thought I stood out as a good candidate, so he recommended that he meet with me for lunch.

I'd already been rejected by so many consulting firms by this time that I hadn't even bothered to sign up to interview with this company. However, I immediately accepted the invitation for lunch that day and proceeded to have a comfortable "non-interview" discussion with this senior leader from Arthur D. Little (ADL, the oldest consulting firm in the world). We talked about life, what mattered to us, why I'd chosen the path I was on, what I'd learned along the way, why I found consulting intriguing, and what we both did for fun. It was a fascinating conversation in which I felt so comfortable in who I was—and who I wasn't—and felt no pressure to have to land a job or nail the interview. It was just a nice conversation between two new acquaintances. That night, I got a call from Walter, and he offered me a job. I couldn't believe it.

Three years later, I was living in Boston, working for ADL, when I got a call from another consulting firm: McKinsey & Company, one of the most well-respected and difficult-to-get-into consulting firms in the world. It was also one of the firms that had rejected me just a few years earlier at UCLA. They were calling back to see what I was up to. It turns out that I'd actually done well enough in my original interview to warrant McKinsey wanting to keep tabs on me to see if I would end up getting work experience and building skills—beyond being able to land a plane on a glacier—that would be useful to McKinsey's consulting clients. The first call went well, and I agreed to re-interview to see if I might be a good fit for a new "customer management" practice that the firm was creating. I had five interviews over the course of two weeks. I'd felt pretty good about making it that far, and I wondered what would happen next.

I remember the evening like it was yesterday. I was staying at the Hilton near Chicago's O'Hare airport and was about to go to sleep when I got a call from soon-to-become-great-friend Marc Singer.

McKinsey wanted to offer me a job to join as an associate. I couldn't believe it. I was about to become a member of the venerable McKinsey & Company! I accepted, and a month or so later, I was starting in McKinsey's Boston office.

Fast-forward several more years and I had moved to San Francisco to support McKinsey's thriving practice working for "dotcom" startups and myriad tech companies that populated the entire West Coast of the U.S. By then, I was married with two children. I was still flying, albeit just for fun rather than for a living. I loved my life, and despite the crazy-long hours and the four-day peak-travel schedule, I was feeling incredibly thankful for how life was unfolding for me.

However, I was also noticing that very few of the people I was encountering seemed to have the same level of inspiration and appreciation for the life they were living as I did. Instead, I was seeing people who were burned out. Most had no hobbies or interesting activities going on at home, and many of the more senior people I looked to as role models were in the process of getting divorced and in general were often not particularly happy or, for that matter, interesting people.

As I reflected on this at the time, I looked back over my prior 20 years and it occurred to me that I'd had the privilege of working with some of the most "successful" people in the world—people who by all visible measures were living the ultimate life. They'd typically gone to the best schools, and many were incredibly accomplished: Olympic athletes, valedictorians, Rhodes Scholars, and C-suite executives. They typically had a substantial income, a nice house, and a luxury car, and their kids often went to the best private schools. On top of that, many of them had accomplished their dreams!

Despite these well-recognized hallmarks of success, many of these individuals were clearly unhappy. They had material possessions, an impressive résumé, and status symbols, but they were not living "a life well lived." Of course, this wasn't true for everyone. I could tell that some people had a real zest for life, energized by the people around them and activities they took part in.

I was perplexed by this. I wondered what differentiated the individuals who found their "true north" and built truly inspiring, fulfilling lives from those who didn't. This question became the basis for creating this book.

Working for several decades in a wide variety of jobs with a broad cross section of people, I've had a unique and privileged opportunity to observe the way people operate, the way they make decisions, and the things they prioritize that lead to vastly differing outcomes. It's these insights that compelled me to distill in this book what I've seen among these individuals and families who have "figured it out" and managed to build a life that is truly inspired and fulfilling.

I've not only written about what I've learned but also live the same principles I've outlined—in a way, serving as my own test case to validate these perspectives. This approach has helped me shape the most meaningful, inspiring, and fulfilling life I can. And it's my passion to help those around me find their true north and do the same.

Darren and his family on vacation in Italy.

What does it mean to be inspired?

To me, inspiration is the feeling I get when the wheels of my plane leave the ground and all the trees become tiny dots below me. It's watching my wife and kids laughing at the dinner table. It's meeting with my colleagues at Cisco and working through tough challenges in creative ways.

Inspiration is the surge of energy coursing through my veins, awakening my senses and filling me with a heightened sense of enthusiasm and motivation. Emotionally, it can take on many forms. Sometimes it's a profound sense of joy, and other times it's a peaceful contentment. I can feel determined, passionate, or creative. Even more than that, I feel like I'm living my purpose, connected to the world around me.

The concept of an inspired life is deeply personal and subjective. It reflects your values, passions, and desires. What lights you up isn't necessarily going to be the same thing that lights me up. In fact, there are 7.8 billion people in this world, and there are just as many versions of what an inspired life looks like.

But no matter what you might want, living an inspired life is rarely easy. If the stars align perfectly, it's possible that you could be presented with the optimal mix of experiences at every turn. But even then, you would need to recognize opportunities when they emerge and then act on them rather than letting them pass you by.

The vast majority of the time, living an inspired life requires an incredible amount of intentionality. You must know what truly lights you up, know what doesn't, and be able to work toward crafting an existence that enables you to get what you need on a regular basis. This work is a lifelong journey—and everything hinges on getting it right.

We see this play out countless times in the people we meet. You know how some people always seems to be in a good mood? They have an unwavering sunny outlook, and any challenges or setbacks they encounter are like water off a duck's back. It's easy to think that these individuals are lucky or that they just have a naturally positive disposition. Though that may be true, chances are that their day-to-day experience lights them up and makes them feel fulfilled. They are living an inspired life.

The opposite can be said for the crotchety people who always seem to have something negative to say. They might deeply dislike their job and have no loving relationships, few friends, and nothing that brings them joy. They aren't hardwired to be irritable; they are simply living a life that is so uninspiring that they struggle on a daily basis.

No one intentionally chooses to live like this, but it happens to all sorts of people. Somewhere along the way, people can lose sight of what really matters to them and make choices that only move them further away from what an ideal life looks like. Before they know it, they're stressed, depressed, anxious, unhealthy, and—of course—uninspired.

We've all found ourselves at least dipping a toe into this end of the swimming pool at one time or another, and it does not feel good.

Personal fulfillment and well-being matter. You don't want this life! You don't want to slog through each day with a rain cloud hanging over your head and no sign of sunny skies ahead.

Instead, your goal should be to engage in meaningful and enriching experiences every day. It might sound Pollyanna-ish to some, but you can be truly delighted by the world around you.

You might argue that this state of being has a lot to do with upholding a positive attitude. There's absolutely truth in this, but it's much easier to be a glass-half-full person when you find joy and fulfillment across numerous areas of your life. That's why if you're intentional about crafting the life you truly want to live, it becomes a virtuous cycle where positive experiences and a positive outlook feed off each other. The challenge lies in cultivating a life that supports this virtuous cycle.

Let's be honest: we're all trying to lead our best life. None of us are out there in the world intentionally losing sight of our true north and making choices that will lead to discontentment, boredom, pain, misery, or regret. Yet sometimes we find ourselves facing those emotions. And more often than not, it's the result of making the wrong choices.

Over the years, I've been afforded an intimate look at how being successful and being fulfilled are not the same thing. Working as a private-jet pilot early in my career, and years later as an executive at some of the world's leading tech and consulting firms, I've had access to rarified environments where I got to know a wide range of aspirational people. From movie stars to entrepreneurs and Fortune 100 leaders who are worth millions, I spent many years with individuals who'd "made it." As we lounged on catamarans in the Caribbean or dined at Michelin-starred restaurants, I expected all these people to be inspired and fulfilled. But many were not. They were often stressed and unhappy; they had no hobbies, their relationships were suffering, and they were certainly not experiencing the joy of having arrived at a place of wealth, status, and power. They'd chased a vision of success that did not align with what mattered most to them, and their happiness suffered because of it.

I'll admit that reflecting on these observations became a near obsession of mine. I just couldn't wrap my head around the massive gap between what "the good life" looks like to others and what it feels like to the person who is actually living it. Perception and reality can be light-years away from each other. I realized that so many people are navigating their existence based on narratives that are not their own.

We are all under immense pressure to aspire to certain hallmarks of success: an impressive job, a beautiful home, and plenty of money, just to name a few. From a young age, these viewpoints become so engrained in our worldview that they turn into an undercurrent, pushing us in a direction that other people think we should travel. We therefore often end up in a place that is less fulfilling than we anticipated. The outcomes we thought would bring us happiness ultimately fall short, and we find ourselves pursuing the wrong things. It doesn't have to be this way.

In the following pages, I show you how simple considerations, strategies, and habits lead to more fulfilling outcomes. You will learn how to break free from other people's narratives about what success looks like and identify what truly lights you up as a unique individual. By targeting nine key principles that have the power to unlock inspiration, you'll be able to home in on the areas that matter most. You'll learn strategies for enacting positive change in your daily life, setting the right goals, and overcoming the fear of the unknown so you can pivot to compelling new experiences.

I encourage you to visit the appendix for worksheets and resources referenced throughout the book. You can also download these on my website, linked in the QR code on the next page.

Whether you're considering a major change in your life's direction, trying to inspire and guide your children, or simply wondering whether you could be more fulfilled, this book is for you. It's never too late to course correct and follow a new path that will make you happier. After all, this is your life, and you are the only person who knows how you can make the most of it.

Darren's son Chris pursuing his true north, which takes place mostly in the mountains.

SCAN ME

CHAPTER 1

What does an inspired life look like to you?

In certain social circles and areas of the world, parents feel enormous pressure to get their kids into a top kindergarten program and elementary school. When I worked in San Francisco, I knew many people who felt this pressure. One colleague in particular sticks out in my mind. When her son was four years old, she had already identified an elementary school she felt would be sure to set him on the best life path. It was a private school that charges a small fortune for enrollment, and it's in such high demand that it's shockingly hard to get a spot. The students come from a privileged background and have parents who are tech executives or successful entrepreneurs, or were "trust-fund kids" themselves. Having a child who attended that school became a sign of status and success, so my colleague had become determined to get her son into that school.

She spent many hours volunteering and getting to know the teachers, faculty, and parents. She participated in the school's fundraising events and donated money with the goal of having her son become a student the following year. At the same time, she developed a strong focus on his academic achievement, an endeavor she attacked with the same rigor she showed at work. It almost seemed like it had turned into a second job for her.

It was clear to me how important it was for her that her son get into this particular kindergarten, but I couldn't help but notice that she was making herself miserable in the process. She was tired, stressed, and distracted. I could only imagine how her four-year-old felt.

Finally, the time came for the little boy to take the kindergarten admissions test. He did his best, but he did not get in. My colleague was devastated. She genuinely thought that her son's chance at a bright future had been knocked down in a single blow. I'm sure it was a huge hit to her ego as well. Watching this, I felt sad for them both.

As I reflected on this experience my colleague had gone through, I couldn't help but wonder what had possibly generated so much intention and anxiety in her efforts to secure such a "coveted spot" in the local kindergarten. I had gone to a public elementary school, middle school, and high school, and I had somehow seemed to turn out fine. I also knew many people who had charted widely differing paths through school, some of whom went to prestigious private schools while others went to schools I'd never heard of. Despite this diversity of educational experiences, there were many examples of people I'd encountered who were living truly inspiring and fulfilling lives. As such, I was taken aback by how distraught my friend was from what to me seemed like only a very minor hiccup along the journey of life.

It occurred to me that my friend was not alone and that many people in our peer group were pursuing very similar paths, focused on securing a tightly defined course through life with perceptions that anything else was akin to abstract failure. They were also often imposing a true north on another person (in many cases, their child) that may or may not have been at all a path that would set that person up for a life of inspiration and fulfillment. There was never any ill intent. Instead, they were driven by a conviction that was typically instilled by their parents, or by input from friends and family, that suggested this was the "right thing to do," whether or not it really was.

Navigating the many choices in life is hard enough without outside influence, and it becomes even more convoluted when you bring other perspectives into the picture. Hundreds of times a day, every day, you are on the receiving end of both direct and indirect messaging about what you should aspire to have and become. Influence is embedded into culture, family expectations, societal norms, conversations with friends, ads on TV, posts on social media, and virtually every other form of communication you can think of.

Even if you don't realize it, these messages can play a significant role in shaping your perceptions and beliefs about happiness and success. Internalizing messages about material wealth, social status, professional achievements, or external validation impacts the choices you make and the goals you set for yourself—both consciously and subconsciously. From childhood through adulthood, you are influenced by standards created by other people, including societal norms, cultural expectations, and prevailing definitions of what it means to live a good life. These forces can sway you in making major life decisions such as what career path to pursue as well as inconsequential choices like what kind of breakfast cereal to buy your kids.

Sometimes, influence is easy to spot: your sister tells you point-blank that your car is a piece of junk and you should be embarrassed to be seen driving it. Other times, influence is much less overt: you watch a luxury-car-dealership commercial that features a happy, prosperous, good-looking family driving off into the sunset together. In either case, these interactions can leave you feeling less satisfied about an area of your life. Even if upgrading your car was not top of mind yesterday, today you're wondering if you should make it a priority. *Maybe you would be happier if you had a nicer car.*

We all battle with these thoughts on a regular basis. If you were to audit all the thoughts that travel through your brain on any given day, I bet you'd find that a large portion of them are related to influence—especially at a subconscious level. This is human nature. We see what's happening in the world around us and benchmark ourselves against what we see; we want to measure up. But the problem with this is that we don't all want the same things. What makes you happy won't necessarily make me happy. That's why it's crucial to have awareness of the pressures and influences that surround you day in and day out and determine which narratives you should toss out the window.

Using the example of the pressure to buy a new car, it could be possible that car ownership doesn't fit into your lifestyle. Perhaps what you really want is to move to New York City to pursue ballet, and you would take the subway everywhere instead of driving. Or maybe you love riding your bike and you would find more fulfillment getting a new job that allows you to ride to work every day. We don't all want the same things. That's what makes life beautiful and interesting.

The first step in working toward crafting a more inspired life is recognizing that you should be pursuing different objectives from everyone around you. Society provides a framework for what a fulfilling life might look like, but it is up to you to critically evaluate these influences and determine your own path. By aligning your definition of success with your authentic self and personal values, you can break free from societal pressures and find a sense of purpose and satisfaction on your own terms.

Define what an inspired life looks like to you

There are many ways to think about living an inspired life. I want to challenge you to go beyond the aspects that might come to mind right away and go deeper. Some of the less-visible elements offer an outsized return on investment. Below is a list of elements that are often tied to being fulfilled in life. Though only some of them are related, they all offer unique value.

As you read through this list, note which ones jump out to you as must-haves, and add any others that might be missing. Though they all might sound great, you'll need to determine which ones are more important than others so that you can establish priorities and goals.

- ➤ **Pursuing passions.** If you're passionate about something, living an inspired life means tapping into that passion in some capacity. Along the same lines, you should give yourself the chance to explore new interests that could turn into passions. Even if this is done as a hobby instead of a paid role, it's how you add layers of richness to your life.

- ➤ **Mastery.** When people hone a skill set and work hard to become excellent at something that aligns with their passions, they often experience a deep sense of gratification, accomplishment, and boost to their self-worth. Becoming great at something has many other rewards as well, as we'll talk about in a later chapter.

- ➤ **Meaningful connections/relationships.** It takes time, work, and intentionality to develop and maintain positive relationships. This is true for partners, immediate family members, extended family members, friends, coworkers, and anyone else in your life.

- ➤ **Being around other people.** This is different from the previous point because we're not necessarily talking about building meaningful relationships. Instead, this point is about sharing a physical space with other people you can interact casually with, rather than being isolated. The pandemic taught us a great deal about loneliness, and many people learned that they aren't meant to sit at home alone every day. If you're someone who needs to get out of the house and interact with strangers, meet with coworkers, or network professionally, this is certainly something to consider when envisioning your ideal life.

➤ **Purpose.** There's nothing quite like knowing that what you're doing is making a difference. People find purpose in many ways, from working for a nonprofit organization to raising children to shoveling snow from a neighbor's driveway. It's oftentimes rooted in altruism, such as volunteering to do community service, but it doesn't have to be. You can find purpose in any job well done—even in just taking care of yourself.

➤ **Home.** The place you reside can be a safe haven that gives you space to recharge, acts as a gathering place for friends and family, and is a source of comfort and security. These benefits don't necessarily correlate with living in an expensive home or owning your own place. It's more about the way your home makes you feel and whether it helps or hinders you in other areas of your life.

➤ **Physical belongings.** Marie Kondo became famous for advising her clients to downsize by asking themselves which of their belongings truly spark joy and getting rid of the rest. This is important to note because some of your physical belongings absolutely play a role in you living an inspired life: your childhood stuffed animal, supplies or equipment you need for your favorite hobby, your favorite shirt that makes you feel like a million bucks every time you wear it. But it's also important to note that the vast majority of your possessions do not impact how fulfilled you are on a daily basis.

➤ **Amount of free time.** Spending all day every day lying in a hammock or on a towel at the beach sounds nice, but for most of us, it would get boring. How much free time to spend how you please would you ideally have on a weekly basis? Understanding what this ideal number looks like can give you a sense of the type of job that could be a good fit for you. For example, if you don't require a lot of free time, you could consider a more demanding job. But if you place a high value on free time, it might be worth it for you to enjoy a simple lifestyle and work fewer hours.

➤ **Autonomy.** Having a sense of control over your choices can go a long way toward driving satisfaction. You can achieve autonomy in many ways, including having few obligations, a flexible job, and a financial safety net.

➤ **Location.** Some people don't have a strong preference for where they reside, while others feel the need to be in a particular country, city, or neighborhood. If family members or friends live nearby, it can certainly improve your quality of life.

➤ **Hobbies/activities that bring you joy.** If surfing lights you up and you can't imagine a life without it, that's a sign you should prioritize this category. You will need to compromise other areas of your life to give your hobby more weight, but it may very well be worth it.

➤ **Personal growth.** Are you continually striving to become a better version of yourself? If you're interested in self-exploration, honing new skills, or lifelong learning, personal growth could be a key part of your ideal life.

➤ **Spirituality.** This can take on many different meanings depending on who you ask, but spirituality is often a major way people find fulfillment, comfort, and community.

➤ **Exercise.** Living an active lifestyle can be a foundational element to staying happy, warding off stress, and feeling confident in your body. Everyone needs regular exercise to stay physically healthy, but for some people, it's a major contributor to their mental health as well. If this sounds like you, make sure to prioritize this part of your life.

➤ **Travel.** There are many ways to see the world, whether on road trips with family, traveling abroad for work, or taking a sabbatical to immerse yourself in a new culture. If you have a travel bug, make sure you're feeding it properly so that it keeps energizing you.

➤ **Adventure.** If you need a little spice and intrigue in your life, adventure could be a key category for you. This can encompass anything from adrenaline sports to exploring a new neighborhood to embracing change in general.

➤ **Stability.** Though some people are energized by change and not knowing what the future holds, others find deep comfort in knowing exactly what to expect. Stability can be the foundation a lot of people need to make progress optimizing other areas of their life.

➤ **Community.** Historically, being a member of a community was a central focus of daily life. People relied on each other for support in nearly every aspect of life, from putting food on the table to raising children to protecting one another. Today, although it's possible to live independently with no outside interaction or support, it can be lonely and isolating. There's an enormous amount of value to be found in being part of a group that shares a common bond or interest. This can be found online, but it's even better when you can connect in person.

Take a few moments to jot down notes about the elements that stand out to you the most. Don't think about what your current reality is, but rather think about what your ideal life would look like if anything were possible. Which elements would play a crucial role in giving you energy, enthusiasm, and a zest for life? Which ones would need to be part of your daily or weekly routine or incorporated a few times a year?

Once you've completed this exercise, it's time to compare your vision with what things are like for you today. Are there elements you identified as being important but are currently lacking for you? Perhaps you're feeling solid about a couple elements, but many are completely missing or neglected. Be as honest as possible with yourself. You might be the picture of success and happiness to others, but how does your life feel to *you*?

If you're sensing a major gap between where you are today and where you'd like to be, don't panic! We all have moments like that. The most important thing is to gain the awareness that you should be pursuing a path to change and start shifting your day-to-day reality closer to your vision for an inspired life. No matter how old you are or how much time and effort you've invested in going a certain direction in life, it's never too late to try something different.

Loree Draude, a good friend of mine, is an excellent example of how a person can reinvent themselves to shape a life that feels more authentic, inspired, and fulfilling. Loree grew up in a conservative military family in the South. Throughout her school years, she loved theater. She would use every opportunity to try out for plays and would always aspire to the lead role. Her parents were supportive and found this energy she had for performing to be "endearing," as most parents would.

However, as Loree was in her teenage years approaching adulthood, it became increasingly clear to her that although her acting passion was endearing to her parents, it certainly wasn't something they would endorse as a career. To the contrary, conversations around "what do you want to be when you grow up?" were always slanted toward far more traditional and predictable careers, including following in her mother and father's footsteps with a career in the military.

It was always curious to Loree that her parents loved art and theater but were very much of the view that such an endeavor was for *other people*—not their daughter Loree.

After much discussion, Loree decided to join the Navy and leave the world of acting behind. She did well, graduating from Officer Candidate School, successfully completing flight training, and becoming a naval aviator. She was ultimately selected to be in a group of the first female aviators to fly combat aircraft aboard an aircraft carrier. Loree spent a decade in the Navy, and while there, she found ways to scratch her acting itch by participating in onboard plays, organizing fun skits, and spending time with others on the ship who shared her interest in entertainment.

Following the Navy, Loree wrestled with what to do next. She applied to film school and got in but got scared about whether it was a "safe enough" option and about what her parents would think. This fear ultimately resulted in her backing out of film school to pursue an MBA at Wharton instead. Upon graduation, Loree stepped into the corporate world, first with Bain & Company, a global management-consulting firm, and from there landed at several startups in Silicon Valley before arriving at Google, where she spent multiple years leading a community-advocacy group. This work eventually led to her taking a key role at Facebook to lead a team focused on creating content to educate business owners. It was the quintessential Silicon Valley career path. Along the way, she got married, had two children, and bought a home in Palo Alto. By most people's standards, Loree was "living the dream."

However, though Loree may have been living someone's dream, it certainly wasn't hers. Each of her jobs required working crazy-long hours. Traffic in the Bay Area is atrocious, so an hour or more each day was spent just going to and from work. And the price of a home in Palo Alto meant that both she and her husband had to work just to make it through each month. On virtually every block in Palo Alto, there's at least one family who has "made it" with a large house, multiple expensive cars, and millions in the bank, so the constant pressure to "keep up" was everywhere.

And all the while, Loree had this nagging feeling that what she was doing wasn't at all aligned with who she was as a person and what she really wanted to do with her life. This feeling and pressure continued to build until one day she finally found the courage to make the life pivot she knew in her heart of hearts she had to make but hadn't yet had the courage to admit to herself.

During her time at Facebook, Loree began working with a career coach, which prompted two highly impactful life changes. For one, it got her thinking about alternative career paths that would have her spending more time in ways that tapped into her natural interests and energy. It also introduced her to the world of career and life coaching, which felt like a great fit to her and she had gotten a taste of when leading diverse teams of sailors in the Navy. She signed up for a coaching course and got certified within a year. This gave her the "landing spot" for leaving her corporate life and embarking on the next stage of her career—one that was far more aligned with things that mattered to her and drew on the energy she had inside her to do something that mattered in the world.

It was during the early days of this newfound career of life coaching when Loree also took on being a yoga instructor and started to form mindsets that would set her up for the next big stage of her life. Fear of failure had been something in the back of her mind her whole life, and her coach had shared with her a view that the word "fail" stands for "first attempt in learning." Her coach said that every failure is a great thing in that it provokes learning and moves a person forward.

This perspective was the foundation of Loree's next big life change, which was to write her own one-person play that she could produce and star in. Talk about a total change in direction from what she was doing before! This idea was a brave and innovative way for Loree to get back to her childhood love of performing and entertaining. It also served as a vehicle for her to tell her story in a way that would inspire her audience to think about how they could shape their own lives in positive ways.

I Feel the Need was launched off-Broadway in New York just as the COVID-19 pandemic was ending. The play received great reviews—winning the U Solo NYC Award—and several months later, Loree was invited to perform for a month at the Edinburgh Fringe Festival in Scotland. This opportunity provided her with the ability to hone her performance and get in front of thousands of people. She followed her Scotland experience with a stint performing in Los Angeles and then settled back in New York. There, she began to take acting lessons, audition for other roles, and continue to provide life coaching to clients around the country. Her son and daughter are now young adults, and her daughter goes to school in New York City, which gives Loree lots of opportunity to see her.

Loree Draude evolved her life from fighter pilot to stage actor.

Today, Loree is fulfilled and happy. Instead of feeling like she's living someone else's vision of success, she's making choices on her own terms. She's come full circle and returned to her original love of art and entertainment while also tapping into a love of helping people succeed. She doesn't exactly know what the next 10 years have in store for her, but that excites her! She's found herself waking up every day doing the things that she wants to do and being the person that she wants to be. She recognizes that perhaps she has less money in her bank than she would have if she'd stayed at Google or Facebook, but she feels more fulfilled.

The way that Loree was able to pivot is something we all can admire. Making those kinds of difficult life decisions can be terrifying! We put a lot on the line hoping for something better. What makes this even harder is when the point before the pivot looks perfectly fine to other people. (Why risk everything when you have so much going for you already?) But if you don't feel like you're living the life that gives you energy and lights you up, it doesn't matter what other people think about it.

Perhaps inspired by her team in Scotland, in my interview with her for this book, she paraphrased Sir William Wallace by reminding me that "everyone dies, so make sure you live the life YOU want to live." That's exactly what this book is about.

One thing I love about Loree's story is that she has shaped her life around numerous elements that matter to her. That's a key aspect to living an inspired life. We are all complex, multifaceted individuals. We can't expect to lead an inspired life by only focusing on one or two dimensions and forgetting about the rest. We need to think holistically.

This is especially important because there will always be highs and lows—no matter who you are. Things will not always go as planned. You might get fired from your dream job, dumped by your partner, or into an accident that leaves you disabled. If all your eggs are in one basket, and that's the basket that gets dropped, it can be devastating. Recovering from a situation like that can take months or even years. But if you invest time and energy into developing many different areas of your life, when something bad happens, it doesn't feel as catastrophic. The same line of thinking can apply when an area of your life turns into a long-term struggle that saps your energy and increases your stress. If you don't have much else going on in your life, those bright spots need to shine even brighter to balance out the darkness. But if your life is full of things that give you little bursts of energy and joy, you won't need to lean on any of them too hard individually.

As you think about what your most inspired life looks like, establish your goals. Write them down now. It's essential to get clear on what you're trying to achieve so that you can begin taking actions that support your goals.

Instead of using others as a benchmark for your happiness, focus on your own aspirations. Beware of getting caught up in external factors, as they will likely leave you feeling unfulfilled. Tune in to yourself, prioritize your own happiness, and identify what truly fills your cup. Rather than constantly asking yourself if you're doing better than everyone around you, it's time to look inward and seek fulfillment on your own terms.

CHAPTER 2

Intentionally intentional

When I was in graduate school, I went to a presentation on campus that was being given by a local pilot, Elwood Schapansky. He worked as a physics professor during the school year and an Alaska bush pilot in the summer. His job was to fly small planes delivering supplies, food, fuel, and people to remote areas of Alaska that are inaccessible via roads or railways. His story was so exciting and unique that I became totally captivated by the sense of adventure it offered. After the presentation was over, I couldn't stop thinking about it. For weeks on end, I found myself daydreaming about what it would be like to experience the same adventures that Elwood had talked about, and I couldn't help but contrast those fantasies with my day-to-day life as an engineering graduate student. After much deliberation and introspection, I decided to put my studies on hold and head north to Alaska in search of an exciting flying job. I never planned on making a career out of it, but I felt that if ever there were a time to take this sort of chance, it was then, before I'd enter the "real job" market.

Although I had many years of flying experience, I was only 22 and knew that I wouldn't necessarily be a shoo-in candidate for most open bush-pilot positions. The majority of flying companies in Alaska only hire pilots who have a lot of Alaska flying experience, and I would be arriving with absolutely none. As such, I knew I would need to work hard to get hired anywhere, highlighting the experience I did have and showing how it would be relevant for what those companies were looking for. Instead of thinking about this work as a single action and getting overwhelmed by the challenges I knew I'd face, I thought about it instead as a large volume (possibly hundreds!) of relatively small and simple actions.

I started by having a friend mail me the Alaska Yellow Pages (for the younger readers, the Yellow Pages, a.k.a. "the phone book," is how people used to contact one another before the internet). I then did a mail merge and sent hundreds of letters to every flying company in Alaska to introduce myself and inquire about open positions. I identified the most interesting companies and sent follow-up letters to them a few weeks later. I made a couple connections, but I didn't have any solid leads yet. I tried calling several of them, but after getting turned down multiple times, I realized I needed to be there in person to have a shot at making this work. So I bought a one-way ticket to Fairbanks and stayed with a friend I'd met a prior summer who happened to live there. I mapped out a route of the companies that hired bush pilots at the Fairbanks airport and began going door-to-door looking for a job. People were friendly, and I was getting a few bites, but most of them were for jobs that weren't nearly as exciting as the type of flying that Elwood had spoken of many months earlier. After talking to a dozen or so companies over several days, I ended up deciding to hitchhike down to Anchorage to knock on more doors.

In Anchorage, I managed to connect with a company that was willing to give me a shot. The manager said that although he had already hired all his pilots for the season, he would train me to be an authorized pilot for them and put me on call. He did warn me that I might not get a single flight all summer, but I was welcome to stand by and see what happened. By that time, I had made hundreds of small actions, and this was the best offer I had received, so I took it.

I invested the next several days in flight training and passed my check-ride, which authorized me to conduct charter flights on my own. At that point, I settled into the reality that I might just be grounded all summer waiting for an opportunity to fly. But at that point, at least I had been certified to fly paying passengers in Alaska, so no matter what happened, I was ahead of where I was when I had arrived in Alaska just a few short weeks earlier. Although the company I was working for had hired all its pilots for the season, it's always impossible to predict how busy any flying season is likely to be. Fortunately for me, the summer I was in Alaska turned out to be a blockbuster year. I had no sooner settled into my role of "just sitting on the couch" when a call came in for a charter to a nearby native Alaskan village. I was the only pilot available and soon found myself enroute to Lime Village to drop off several passengers. When I returned a few hours later, there was another charter that had come in, so I headed right back out to take it. I ended up flying virtually every day that summer and saw more of the state than the majority of Alaskans who live there their entire lives get to.

Being a bush pilot was exactly the adventure I was seeking. Every morning, I woke up excited to see where the day would take me, and every night, I fell asleep almost instantly, feeling satisfied with what I'd experienced. That summer, I was, without a doubt, living my most inspired life.

This experience did not fall into my lap. I'd worked my ass off to get it. Thinking back to all the actions I took, I realize it might sound a bit obsessive—or even crazy. But it worked. I was bound and determined to become a bush pilot that summer, so I became radically intentional.

This is what it often takes to craft your most inspired life. Sometimes you get lucky, and opportunities pop up without any effort, but you can't count on that. Instead, driving real change in your life takes a tremendous amount of intentionality. What got you here will not get you there. You will need to take different actions, and it might feel foreign, uncomfortable, and even scary. But if you keep your vision for an inspired life front and center in your mind, it will help provide the energy and courage you need for making real progress.

Darren on the job as a bush pilot in Alaska. (Shotguns were required safety equipment given the prevalence of bears.)

Create a road map

Exercise: If you're going to focus on intentionality, you need to get hyper specific on the outcomes you want to achieve and the actions that will support those outcomes. Think about the vision you created in the last chapter. For each of the goals you identified, answer the following questions. For an electronic, editable version of this exercise, scan the QR code in the introduction.

➤ What is a long-term outcome you want to achieve?

➤ Why do you want to achieve that outcome?

➤ What are the emotions you associate with that outcome?

➤ What are some short-term outcomes that would help you make progress toward achieving the long-term outcome?

➤ What are actions you will need to take to achieve both short- and long-term outcomes?

This road map will become your guide over the coming months and potentially beyond. You should refer back to it regularly to stay on track.

It's important to note that this road map will work for you in the short term, but it is not meant to be a static plan you will follow for the rest of your life. That's because what you want today might not be what you want in a year, five years, or 20 years. As you have new experiences and grow as a human being, you will go through a journey of self-discovery. You might find out that there are other, more desirable paths to reaching the outcomes you've identified, or you might realize that you want to go after different outcomes altogether. All this is not only perfectly acceptable but also expected.

Dr. Colleen Cira is a psychologist who has worked with many individuals over the years, and she has seen firsthand how going into autopilot has a negative impact on mental health. She says that people tend to get into a mode where they do what they are expected to do and sleepwalk into choices rather than taking the time to stop and question their options. Instead of following the most rewarding, authentic path, they settle for the one of least resistance. This is how people wake up middle-aged and wonder how they got there.

When you establish your vision for living an inspired life, you can't just set it and fall back asleep. If you do, you might find yourself following a true-north plan that no longer suits you. This is just as bad as adhering to a plan someone else created for you or giving in to societal pressure. To safeguard against this, Dr. Cira recommends practicing present-moment awareness "as much as humanly possible."[1] Actively assess how you feel about your progress, the options presented to you, and the choices you have made. Give yourself room to be agile and be willing to change your mind.

When it's time for a change in direction, create new goals and get rid of those that no longer serve you. Simply go through the afore-mentioned list of questions to keep your road map up to date.

Actions

Now that you've hashed out a basic plan to reach your desired out-comes and identified the actions you can take to drive progress, there are a few key things you should know.

Tiny steps forward add up. As you navigate from one place to another, every step forward gets you closer to your destination. Sometimes it might feel like the little things don't matter, but that simply isn't true. It's often the case that one small action will have a vastly outsized impact. Unfortunately, you can't see into the future to know now which actions will end up altering your trajectory down the road! With that in mind, you can consider action as a volume game. Every person you network with, every article you read, and every time you practice honing your skills have the power to change your future. The more actions you take, the better positioned you will be to reach your goals. Improving just a tiny bit every single day is enough to create a long-term transformation. Keep plugging away and you will get to where you want to be. The key is to be conscious of your daily actions and to remember to ask yourself, "Are the actions I'm taking today getting me any closer to my goal?" As long as you have far more yeses than nos, then you're likely in good shape.

Form good habits. Knowing that you will be taking hundreds—if not thousands—of actions over your lifetime to craft your most inspired life, you cannot underestimate the importance of developing good habits. This can be the difference between achieving your goal and never quite getting there. I highly recommend reading *Atomic Habits* by

James Clear. This book presents numerous strategies for making small, consistent action a part of your everyday life. As James describes, the key to forming a new habit is to "make the action obvious, make it attractive, make it easy, and make it satisfying."[2] James has a treasure trove of good frameworks and tips for bringing this to life, and, at the core, his message is largely around the idea that actions matter. If you can make an action a habit, then taking action over time becomes a lot easier. If you can make a habit attractive or satisfying, it becomes much easier to sustain progress over time. It's actually a pretty simple concept—and it works—but it takes intentionality to do it.

Some actions are procrastination. I went kiteboarding a while back in Mexico, and my buddy let me stay at his vacation house. He let me know that another guy was currently living there and that we would have no problems getting along. When I got to the house, we started chatting, and I asked what had brought him to Mexico. He told me he'd come down from the U.S. to study cryptocurrency with the goal of becoming a crypto guru. I told him I thought it was a cool idea, and I asked what he was doing to become an expert. When he revealed that he usually spends time listening to podcasts, reading, and trying to figure out next steps, I figured that he was early on in his journey and had maybe been at it for a month or so. In reality, he had been living there and working on it for a year. A whole year! And he hadn't even traded a single bit of cryptocurrency; he was just "studying it."

Sometimes it can feel like you're making progress toward your goal when you're actually just procrastinating by focusing on easy tasks that don't intimidate you and drawing them out longer than necessary to delay getting to the harder parts of the process. This is not productive. No one wants to just "be busy" and have their actions not really make a difference in getting them to their desired outcome, yet so many people get stuck in that spot. It's like an athlete who has never actually gotten on the field. You can only learn so much in practice. At some point, you have to get in the game if you want to keep learning and growing. There's truly no way around it. Yes, it's scarier to play in a real game than putz around during practice, but it's the only way you can truly move forward. In general, "getting in the game" means you interact with other people who are doing the thing you want to do and start to actually do that thing as well, even if you're not very good at it when you start. It's the "doing" that builds the experiences that you'll need to turn your goals into reality.

Don't go backward. You need to be aware of the actions that are moving you further away from where you want to be. For example, if you want to improve your health, and you are smoking a pack of cigarettes and eating a pint of ice cream every day, you're probably going in the wrong direction—unless you used to smoke two packs and eat two pints of ice cream a day, in which case you are going in the right direction, albeit slowly! Ideally, you will recognize in real time when you make a choice that is inconsistent with your goals. Sometimes you will do it intentionally, and it's not an issue (a scoop of ice cream every now and then never hurt anyone). But a problem arises when you make those kinds of choices without realizing that you're slowly sabotaging yourself.

Another type of sabotage people often experience is a version of giving up too early. When they veer off track a little bit, they think all is lost (e.g., "I already ruined my diet today, so why not keep eating whatever I want?"). The answer is pretty obvious when you aren't in the thick of it, but if you're already feeling down about yourself, you might feel like your choices don't matter because you were never going to reach your goal in the first place.

Make no mistake: your efforts matter. All of them. Everything you do can either bring you closer to leading your most inspired life or take you further away from it. Many actions seem inconsequential—and as one-off events, maybe they are. But let me tell you: even tiny steps backward have a way of adding up.

To safeguard against this, I ask myself on a fairly regular basis, "Are the actions I'm taking consistent with the outcome I want to achieve?" If they are, then great; I just need to keep doing them. If they're not, I force myself to confront that and make a change. All too often, I listen to people tell me the great plans they have for their life but see huge inconsistencies between the stated outcomes they want to achieve and the actions they take on a regular basis. It's so important to be aware of this and to call yourself on it whenever you notice any sort of inconsistency between desired outcomes and the actions you're taking.

Make a positive impact. It's a well-researched fact that one of the key elements of feeling inspired and fulfilled in your life is to know that what you're doing and who you're being "matter." People need to know that there's a purpose to what they're doing, and there's no better way to create a sense of purpose than to help others. Perhaps the best litmus test for your actions is to ask yourself whether you are making the world a better place than how you found it. This doesn't have to mean curing cancer or solving the climate-change crisis. It can be as simple as showing kindness, empathy, and compassion to others and making someone else's life just a little bit better. This is important to keep in mind as you focus on your own personal goals. Do not approach this work without thinking about the greater impact on the world around you. Living an inspired life should not come at a cost to others. Think about how you can help people as you travel along your journey, and as much as possible, help others rise up with you.

Intentionally intentional   25

Mindset

When it comes to driving outcomes, actions are important. But I'd be remiss if I didn't talk about mindset. That's because behind every action are the thoughts and beliefs that lead you to take the action:

Beliefs -> Thoughts -> Actions -> Outcomes

Outcomes are a result of actions; actions are a result of thoughts; thoughts are a result of beliefs. To drive different outcomes, you will need to take different actions and have different thoughts and beliefs. This might sound simple, but I'm essentially telling you that you will need to make changes at a core level.

For example, if you want to learn how to play the guitar, there could be many actions you would need to take:

- ➤ Buy / rent / borrow a guitar
- ➤ Watch online tutorials
- ➤ Learn to read music
- ➤ Sign up for private or group lessons
- ➤ Get access to sheet music
- ➤ Carve out regular time to practice
- ➤ Spend time practicing

These actions take work, and potentially some financial investment, but none of them seem too difficult or complicated, right? The harder part is what goes on inside your head. The voice that tells you you'll never be a legitimate musician, so why even bother? Or that you'll embarrass yourself by signing up for lessons and struggling through them in front of strangers. Or that if you tell any of your friends or family members about your goal of learning to play guitar, they will think it's a silly waste of time.

When you hold these kinds of beliefs, and have these sorts of thoughts swirling through your head, do you think it's likely that you'll take the actions you need to take in order to achieve the outcome you want? Nope. It's more likely that you will just continue doing what you've been doing instead of trying anything new. And if you do step outside your comfort zone, you won't have the fortitude to keep going if you hit adversity, which you undoubtedly will at some point.

That voice inside your head that talks down to you is the sound of fear—and it does not have your best interest at heart. If you listen to it discourage you and feed your imposter syndrome (when you doubt your own abilities and feel like you're a fraud), you will not go through with the actions that will drive the outcomes you want. That voice will cause you to live small because you feel insecure.

That's why, before we dig into building a road map for how to get to your goals, we need to talk about mindset. To live your most inspired life, you will need to shift your thinking. This is something you will work on up front, but you can't just do it once and check a box. Upholding an empowered mindset is an advanced skill that people must continuously work on their entire lives. Even the most accomplished, successful individuals, no matter the industry, have moments when they question themselves and their abilities. It's natural to have those thoughts, but the key is to notice them and then release them from your mind.

Here are a few of the best strategies for getting into a good headspace:

Identify the source of your insecurities. We all have our own ideas of how we fail to measure up in certain areas. These beliefs play a major role in our behavior because they cause us to hold back instead of being bold. If you can be honest with yourself and name your insecurities, you'll have a good starting point for addressing—and ultimately conquering—them.

Many insecurities stem from childhood or adolescence, when we are most impressionable. This is also an age range when kindness and tact have not yet been fully developed and hurtful comments run rampant. Maybe someone told you as kid that you have a huge nose, you're a terrible artist, or you look awkward when you run. Those criticisms sometimes have a way of taking root in your brain. Before long, some offhand comments from a random person become things you actually take to heart and believe about yourself. Maybe you're 50 years old and have always wanted to try your hand at watercolor painting but never have because you still feel like the 8-year-old who got laughed at by classmates for drawing a vase of flowers that looked like a brown puddle.

When you're able to identify the source of your insecurities, you can challenge them. In doing so, you're likely to find that a lot of your insecurities were formed years ago and have very little to do with who you are today. Yet chances are the people who gave you negative feedback wouldn't even remember making those comments!

If you do find a hint of truth in an insecurity, you might realize that you've blown it way out of proportion from reality. No one is perfect, or even good at everything—especially in the beginning before they've practiced. If it matters to you to become better at something, you can work toward making progress. In either case, it's time to make a conscious effort to free yourself from limiting beliefs and gain more confidence in yourself.

Be optimistic. You get to choose whether the glass is half empty or half full. It can take conscious practice to develop the muscle that automatically sees every glass as half full—but it's something you can control. It's important to exercise this muscle because life will not always go the way you would ideally like. Bad things will happen from time to time, and if you have trouble being optimistic, you could end up in a negative spiral. To protect yourself from this, you can practice optimism by starting small. If you find yourself being bothered by minor inconveniences or annoyances, take a step back and ask yourself how much it matters in the grand scheme. If it's barely a blip on the radar, try not to focus on it. Instead, think about all the positive aspects. Practice gratitude by not only taking mental note of what you're thankful for but writing it down. The more often you do this, the more naturally you will gain an optimistic perspective. Having a positive attitude can go a long way in shaping your reality in a way that aligns with your vision for an inspired life.

Do not compare yourself to others. Theodore Roosevelt wisely said that comparison is the thief of joy. When we measure ourselves against others, we tend to focus on what we lack rather than appreciating our own unique qualities and accomplishments.

In a world dominated by social media and constant connectivity, there will always be plenty of successful, beautiful, happy people who are on lavish vacations, winning achievement awards, or looking flawless in a swimsuit. These are their high points, but it's hard not to compare them with whatever we're doing in the moment, which is usually much more mundane. Comparison is a pervasive and detrimental habit that creates unrealistic standards and a cycle of dissatisfaction, inadequacy, and self-doubt. Instead of finding joy in our own journey, we can easily become consumed by envy and a drive to match or exceed the achievements of others. This mindset is not conducive to living an inspired life. Competition can be healthy and motivating in certain contexts, but constantly comparing ourselves to others often leaves us feeling "less than," which is unhealthy.

Just as importantly, comparison often distracts you from what really matters to you for living a fulfilled life. Instead of staying focused on the elements you identified in the previous chapter, you're suddenly thinking about superficial or material things that could give you a quick hit of joy or a boost to your ego but won't support you in achieving your long-term goals.

When you feel yourself starting to go down the comparison rabbit hole, take a step back. If you're consuming media that's setting you off, whether it's watching TV, reading a magazine, or scrolling through social media, take a break and do something else. Remind yourself of everything you have going for you. Take time to recenter yourself on your main priorities and goals.

Visualize your success. Visualization, also known as mental imagery or mental rehearsal, is a technique that involves creating detailed mental images of your desired outcomes or goals. It is a well-known and highly regarded strategy for upholding an empowered mindset and boosting performance, especially in high-pressure situations. You see athletes in virtually every sport doing this before games. They put on their headphones and picture going out there and doing their job successfully. They visualize themselves going through the actions they are about to take and feeling the emotions they will experience when they take them in the game. This kind of mental rehearsal has a wide range of benefits:

> **Neuroplasticity.** Repeatedly visualizing successful outcomes can influence the brain's neuroplasticity, strengthening neural pathways associated with confidence and success.

> **Self-efficacy.** As you repeatedly imagine yourself succeeding, your belief in your capabilities grows, leading to more determined efforts in real life.

> **Reduced anxiety.** By mentally rehearsing positive scenarios, you become more accustomed to the situation, making it feel less intimidating. This can reduce performance-related anxiety and stress.

➤ **Focus and concentration.** When you train your mind to pay attention to relevant details and scenarios, it can improve your ability to stay focused when you encounter obstacles in real life.

Try visualization for yourself! You can use it in virtually any scenario, whether it's giving a presentation to clients, having a tough conversation with your boss, or acing an interview. Picture yourself in a state of mastery, expertly handling any challenges that arise, and revel in how good it feels. The more you practice this, the more mentally and emotionally prepared you will feel.

In the end, learning to control the thoughts in your head, and establishing the right mindset for success, is one of the most powerful and sustaining capabilities you will invest in. Unfortunately, your mind will often look for things that can hurt you and then over-amplify the things it finds, which can be enough to stop you from moving forward. Some things, of course, can hurt you—and your mind tries to help you avoid those things—but other things might just have you feeling insecure in front of others such that you might "look bad" or "perform worse," and your mind unfortunately treats these outcomes as equally risky. It's why a shockingly large number of people fear speaking in front of a large audience far more than they fear death. It's irrational, but it's real. As such, recognizing that your mind is not always your best friend when it comes to living an inspired life, and practicing putting stories in your head that provoke action rather than resist it, is enormously powerful.

The beautiful thing about mindset is that you get to choose what stories you tell yourself. So why not choose stories that motivate the actions you'd like to take? A very simple example of this can be conveyed in the following scenario: You're driving home from work and the person behind you is obviously impatient. As you approach a lane merge, they race around to get in front of you. How do you react? One story you could tell yourself is that this person is a jerk, they shouldn't be allowed to get away with such behavior, and they need to be taught a lesson. If that's the story you create in your head, you can imagine the actions you're about to take. You decide to tailgate them, and perhaps at the next opportunity, you'll make sure to get back in front of them. The is likely to only lead to a bad outcome.

What if you created an alternative story: The person behind you has had a lousy day at work. Their child is waiting at school to be picked up and they're running 30 minutes late. They're stressed because things aren't great on the home front and the pressure of all this is overwhelming, and they just want to get their child and get them home safely. If that's the story you tell yourself, what kind of actions might you take? For one, you'd likely feel a bit of empathy for that person. Second, you'd likely not chase after them to "teach them a lesson." You might even feel a bit of gratitude for the fact that you're not having as bad a day as they appear to be having.

Now, the key to this is that you don't actually know which of these stories is true, which is why it's so powerful. It doesn't matter! By choosing the second story, you drive a mindset and associated behaviors that result in a better outcome for that situation. You can apply this approach over and over in ways that cause you to take actions that are consistent with outcomes you want to see for yourself.

Measure and track your progress

What gets measured gets managed. Now that your goals and action plan are written down, it will be easy for you to track and assess your progress. Take notes on the actions you've taken and what you've learned. Just as importantly, record how you are feeling. Are you happier? Less stressed? Do you feel like you're living a more authentic life? Have you increased your ability to make a positive impact? All these factors matter, but they are less visible and often overlooked when evaluating personal progress. Don't become so goal oriented that you lose sight of why you're setting off on this path in the first place. You are crafting *your* most inspired life, not someone else's.

Also recognize that this is a marathon, not a sprint. Though it's good to approach change with enthusiasm and passion, it's equally important to give yourself grace if it takes longer than you hoped to reach your goals. As long as you are practicing self-awareness and intentionality, and adjusting your mindset and actions accordingly, you are moving in the right direction.

Lastly, remember the old adage that "it's the journey, not the destination, that matters." This is quite a powerful concept. Though the destination (the goal, or outcome) of course is important for serving as the catalyst for action and creating a level of motivation and excitement, the journey is where you'll spend most of your time. If you're intentional on your journey, you'll find reward in that alone. In fact, as I think about living an inspired and fulfilling life, the concept of fulfillment speaks to the satisfaction I have from the journey already completed, and the concept of being inspired speaks to the excitement about the journey ahead. The two go together and are incredibly powerful sources of energy that feed on each other to help us achieve great things.

CHAPTER 3

It's who you know

When I was entering my second year of business school at ULCA, my friend Johnna heard about an opportunity to lead the MBA orientation program for first-year students. School administrators were going to pick two students—a guy and a gal—who would be instrumental in shaping the information presented to the incoming class. Johnna told me that the volunteer role would culminate in leading the week-long welcome program for the incoming class of more than 300 students. Seven other pairs had already submitted their names, and she wanted us to submit too. Always positive and optimistic, she said it was an excellent opportunity to try our leadership skills, meet new people, and have fun in the process.

I shot her down immediately. As an introvert, the idea of being onstage in front of 300 people scared me. I pictured all of them staring up at me, judging my every move. What if I couldn't remember what to say? Even if I had cue cards and were able to deliver the information, I doubted that anyone would want to hear it from me. I knew some of the other students who applied for this volunteer role, and they were a lot higher profile than I was. They were extroverted and had no trouble striking up a conversation with anyone. I could picture them having fun with the audience, getting them excited about starting business school, and having the kind of rah-rah attitude that was perfect for being on stage. Johnna was right that it was a good leadership opportunity for someone—but that person was certainly not me.

I thought the conversation was over, but she wouldn't let up. Johnna kept saying that she knew we would do such a great job, and couldn't I just give it a chance? She asked me over and over for days. Finally, I said yes. Not because I wanted to do it, but because I thought there was zero chance we would be selected, given our competition.

Imagine everyone's surprise when Johnna and I were chosen. "Oh shit!" I thought. What did I get myself into?

Johnna and I spent that whole summer working with the faculty and the dean to create a seven-day orientation program for first-year business-school students. It was challenging, but I actually did enjoy it. When orientation week came, Johnna and I were fully prepared. I was nervous on stage at the opening session, but it ended up going so much better than I'd expected! I had my script, and I did what I was supposed to do. And although my delivery wasn't perfect, it went well— and I had fun! The rest of the week was equally successful. Despite being nervous throughout the entire event, I'd managed to show up alongside Johnna and lead our group of volunteer students to deliver an inspiring orientation for the incoming first-year MBA students.

Fast-forward a few months and I get a message out of the blue from the dean asking me if I had time for lunch with a fellow who was visiting the school. The individual was Walter Ulrich, the lead West Coast partner at the global management-consulting firm Arthur D. Little. He was on campus to interview students for a full-time job opening, and his lunch hour was free. He had asked the dean whether there was anyone in the second-year class he felt he should meet with. Surprisingly, the dean suggested me and then reached out to let me know about the opportunity. This wasn't a meeting I had asked for, and it was structured as a casual conversation so there wasn't any pressure on me other than to show up and have a nice lunch with this individual.

Graduation was on the horizon for me, and I had already started applying for consulting jobs. But I hadn't had any offers yet and was unclear what options I'd likely have given that my background relative to my classmates was not nearly as impressive, at least in my mind. (I had gone to public schools; I had never worked for a brand-name company; I wasn't an all-star athlete; and I'd never been a class president or similar. All my classmates seemed to have one or more of those attributes.) As such, although I was intrigued about having lunch with this senior executive, I was already resigned at that point that consulting likely wasn't going to be a career path for me.

Walter and I had a very nice lunch and chatted about all kinds of things. He wanted to know what motivated me and seemed intrigued about my flying background and the eclectic mix of jobs I'd had during and after college. It was an easy and friendly lunch conversation, and it felt like we hit it off. I left the meeting not thinking much of it, other than that Walter was a nice guy and had a lot of interesting stories and experiences. You can imagine my surprise when the next day, Walter extended an offer to me to work at Arthur D. Little in Boston. Naturally, I was surprised and excited. Overnight, I had stumbled into a new career path at a brand-name company that would give me an opportunity to see the world, learn new skills, and double my pre-MBA salary. So of course, I said yes!

This first job out of business school went swimmingly, and it gave me the experience I needed to eventually get a job with McKinsey & Company, one of the top consulting firms in the world. This role opened many other doors for me, including going on to work at Google and then in an executive role at Cisco.

My entire professional trajectory was shaped by a single lunch meeting. And the only reason I had that lunch meeting was because the dean had gotten to know me over the summer when I was working on the orientation program. Johnna told me that the orientation leader role would be a good opportunity to make connections, but it never occurred to me that it would change the course of my life. It all feels very serendipitous now, but that's the power of having a network of friends and supporters.

Close relationships

More often than not, relationships are what open doors and create opportunities that allow you to step into an inspired life. That's the reasoning behind the adage "it's not what you know; it's who you know." Although this saying certainly discounts the importance of having knowledge and skill, it speaks to the fact that relationships are often the catalyst for driving change.

Sometimes chance encounters can be life-changing, but close relationships undoubtably impact us at the core. Jim Rohn, who was a highly successful personal-development coach, used to say that we are the average of the five people we spend the most time with. This theory leverages the law of averages, meaning that the likely result of any situation will be the average of all outcomes. When it comes to close relationships, this theory makes a lot of sense because people are heavily influenced by those around them.

Earlier in this book, we talked about how important it is to think for yourself and not let others shape your views on what it means to live an inspired life. The people you spend the most time with have the power to influence you the most, so it's especially important to surround yourself with people who nudge your mindset and behavior in a direction that aligns with your goals.

Exercise: Your top five

This exercise will give you valuable insight into the dynamics of your closest relationships and help you determine whether they are helping or hindering your efforts to live a more inspired life.

Identify your top five: Write down the names of the five individuals you spend the most time with currently. These people could be family members, friends, or colleagues. Note that you might have actively chosen to spend a lot of time with these people, but it's just as likely that some of them are in your life due to chance or circumstance (e.g., maybe you spend most of your waking hours alongside the coworker you share an office with or your partner's family members).

Reflect: For each person on your list, answer the following questions:

➤ What qualities and characteristics do they possess?

➤ How do they generally affect your mindset, attitude, and overall mood?

➤ Do they support your personal growth and goals? If so, how?

➤ Are their values and beliefs aligned with yours? If not, in what ways do they differ?

➤ Are they individuals who help you be a better you (learn new skills, meet inspiring people, push past your natural insecurities)?

Assess: Take a step back and consider the overall balance of positive and negative impacts on your life from these five individuals. Are the positive influences outweighing the negative ones? Are there any relationships that seem to be predominantly negative or hindering?

Take action: Sometimes people feel like they are stuck in unhealthy relationships that they can't get out of. But that's rarely true. Everyone has the power to make conscious choices about the relationships they cultivate. If someone in your top five is consistently negative or detrimental in your efforts to live an inspired life, how can you begin to distance yourself from that person or minimize the impact they have on you? This doesn't mean you have to officially call it quits with a friend or burn a bridge at work, but you can certainly choose to become less available.

On the flip side, think about your most supportive and uplifting relationships and determine how you can nurture and strengthen those connections. How can you create time and space for more meaningful conversations and fun?

To take it a step further, you should also identify opportunities to expand your network and seek out new relationships with individuals who uplift, inspire, and support your growth. If they deserve a spot in your top five, figure out how to bring them into your inner circle.

As The Beatles told us back in 1967, it's much easier to *get by with a little help from our friends.* When you surround yourself with people who support your aspirations to live a more inspired life, you will make progress faster and it will undoubtedly be more enjoyable.

Role models, mentors, and sponsors

Ethan Martin is just as obsessed with flying as I am. We met in 2017 and instantly connected over our common interest. Ethan founded the Aviation Community Foundation (ACF), which exposes kids from underserved communities to leaders in the aviation industry. Students of all ages get a chance to speak with pilots and get exposure to the many dimensions of aviation, which helps them to understand the many types of jobs that are out there and what they would need to do to pursue that career track. This enables kids to see a path forward that they otherwise would not have known was possible.

Another key aspect of ACF is that it serves as a mentorship opportunity where students can build relationships with aviation professionals who care about their success. Ethan is especially passionate about this part of the program. He knows how important it is for kids to have role models they can look up to. But it isn't just about knowing successful adults; it's also about knowing adults who are working in the industries that kids are interested in pursuing. Some career paths, such as aviation, are a bit more obscure than others. There are fewer people working in the industry, so kids are less likely to meet those professionals organically. ACF brings the aviation industry to kids so they can get the exposure that might spark their interest in flying. This is also a win for the industry, which tends to lack a solid pipeline of qualified candidates to fill open positions.

Kenneth Morris is executive director at ACF, and he grew up like so many of the kids he helps today. Being from inner-city Houston, one of the most dangerous areas of the country, he struggled to see an inspiring path ahead of him, especially when it came to getting a good job. The conversations of the "five people he spent the most time with" were typically about becoming a professional basketball player or selling drugs. This was the extent of what he could see as a possible future—and he wasn't very good at basketball, so his future wasn't looking particularly inspiring. One day, a recruiter for the Coast Guard came by his high school and piqued his interest in the armed services. He ended up joining the Navy, and he scored so high on his entrance exam that he was placed in the aviation sector and began training as an aviation specialist. It was a whole new world opening up to him. He'd always wondered if he would find a career path that he could be passionate about, and he found it flying in the Navy. He looked up to the people he served with, and they treated him with respect. He knew then how valuable that experience was in charting the right course for his life.

Kenneth's experience drove home the idea that you have to "see it to be it" and that so many individuals don't know what they don't

Kenneth Morris pulled himself out of the Houston projects and now inspires people around the world to pursue their dreams.

know about potential paths in life. He was lucky enough to have the Coast Guard come by that one fateful day and expose him to an alternative path, and it transformed the course of his life. Today, he works hard to bring that same experience to kids through ACF.

I have been fortunate enough to volunteer with ACF by speaking at events, coaching ACF members, and participating in ACF strategic-planning sessions. It's an excellent organization that is rooted in one of the most important aspects of living an inspired life: forming positive relationships.

As a society, we seem to understand that kids need exposure to positive role models and mentors, but the truth is that this need doesn't just vanish in adulthood. We all need people we can look up to in various ways.

Sometimes the idea of having role models as an adult seems cheesy or overly simplistic. After all, no one is perfect, so why bother putting anyone on a pedestal?

I can see the logic in choosing not to idolize a person for every aspect of their life, but if we refuse to look to anyone as a role model, we're missing out big time. It's often much easier to follow someone's example than it is to reinvent the wheel every time we try something for the first time. That's why I recommend finding role models for specific facets of life.

As you're thinking about how to craft a life that has various dimensions that inspire you, it's helpful to look out into the world and find people who have similar priorities and passions. They don't have to be good at everything that matters to you, but if they are further along in their journey in a single facet of life that interests you, it could be smart to look at them as a role model. For example, maybe you know a colleague who is unfailingly cool under pressure, and you hope to become more like that. Or your friend's sister has a unique parenting style you want to emulate. Or maybe you randomly came across an expert at home remodeling on YouTube and aspire to level up your DIY skills. All three of these individuals could be your role models at the same time! It doesn't matter if you don't agree with their politics, the kind of music they listen to, or what they choose to spend their money on. You don't have to like—or even know—everything about them. But if you can identify one single thing they do exceptionally well that inspires you, why not look to them for your own personal growth and development?

When you see people achieving growth or success in an area that interests you, it provides a real-life example of what's possible. Having tangible evidence that your aspirations are attainable makes a huge difference in squashing any limiting beliefs or self-doubts you might have. Witnessing someone doing what you want to do also helps you further expand and define what an inspired life looks like for you—at least in one dimension. You might get validation that you're heading in the right direction, or you might see that you want to go after things in a slightly different way. Having that awareness is helpful for guiding you down the right path.

Beyond having role models you can look to for inspiration, it's also important to have mentors. Like role models, these individuals have achieved a level of success in a certain area you admire. But they take the inspiration a step forward by providing support to you in a way that helps guide your path forward. People often become a mentor after they have been your role model. For example, maybe you look up to your professor or manager and begin to ask for their advice in specific areas. They share their knowledge with you, and you build a level of rapport. Over time, they become more invested in your personal growth and success, and you continue to welcome their additional support.

Sometimes these kinds of relationships develop organically, and other times people directly ask whether someone will mentor them. Both routes are common, so don't be shy about pursuing them! Mentorships can be highly beneficial and rewarding for both parties. The mentee gains valuable insight to help them kick-start their progress, and the mentor often finds deep fulfillment in helping someone avoid the same mistakes they once made. As long as a mentee is respectful of their mentor's time, the relationship is usually smooth sailing.

You might have also heard of having a sponsor, which takes the concept of mentoring a step further. A sponsor is someone you have developed a trusted relationship with who is willing to go the extra mile to advocate for you. Instead of just getting insight and advice on how to improve your skills so you can get that job you want, a sponsor will proactively leverage their network to introduce you to the right people to help open up opportunities for you. They believe in you so much that they put their own reputation on the line to recommend you to others and help open doors.

Although having a sponsor can feel like you won a golden ticket, in reality, you can't achieve that sort of relationship without hard work. It often takes years of consistent effort and solid output to develop the level of likeability and trust that is needed for a sponsor to put their neck on the line for you.

As you're thinking about developing relationships with people who inspire you, it's important to realize that you will get far better outcomes if you are intentional about crafting your network. For example, if you want to start your own business, it would be highly beneficial for you to know other entrepreneurs you could talk shop with and learn from. You might randomly meet business owners in your community, but you can accelerate the process by joining small-business networking groups.

It's amazing how the stars can magically align and present you with the exact person you want to meet, but I can tell you with certainty that this happens much more often when you are already connected in a certain space. When people know you're interested in learning more about something or boosting your skills in a specific area, they will proactively introduce you to other people in their network. But if you have six degrees of separation between yourself and the people you might like to meet, your stars will not align as often. You need to get yourself closer to other people in order for the magic to start happening. Whatever it is that inspires you, figure out how to start meeting more people who are further along in that journey. Being proactive makes all the difference.

With all this talk about knowing the right people and understanding how relationships can be beneficial, I would be remiss if I didn't openly address the fact that relationships should not be transactional. As you work to meet more people and build relationships, it can't be purely in the service of seeking out opportunities. You never want someone to feel like the only reason you're interested in talking to them is because you want them to do something for you. Approaching relationships in this manner is hurtful and narcissistic, and it will take you further away from leading the life you want to live. Conversely, finding ways to contribute back to the people who contribute to you pays huge dividends. Offering your advice to them wherever you have some to give, or making introductions between others you know, or simply serving as a sounding board and someone who seeks to help another be a "better version of themselves" amplifies the strength of every relationship you have.

Relationships also bring joy and fulfillment in themselves. When you connect with likeminded individuals who share your passions and interests, your life will develop an even greater sense of richness. But ultimately, the biggest reward comes when you can reach back and help others who aren't as far along as you are and become their mentor—and potentially their sponsor—to help them forge an inspired and fulfilling life. Even if you still feel like you have a long way to go, there will always be people who look up to you and admire how far you've already gone.

How to meet your role models

I'm going to let you in on a secret. (OK, you might already know this, but even if you do, you should probably be doing it more often!) If you look up to someone you don't know in real life, you can reach out to them and try to get to know them. These individuals can be people you came across on LinkedIn or TikTok or someone you've admired for so long you don't even recall how you first heard about them. They can also be speakers at conferences you attend, authors of your favorite books, or notable people in your community. If you admire someone and the prospect of talking to them in real life excites you, you should consider talking to them. Of course, you can set your sights high and aim for celebrities, business moguls, and global influencers, but just keep in mind that A-listers obviously get a lot more people contacting them about all kinds of things, and your message is more likely to get lost in the shuffle than if you were to contact, say, a well-respected professor at your alma matter. That doesn't mean you shouldn't try to connect with role models, regardless of their state in life, but recognize that some individuals will be more challenging to connect with than others. That's OK—and expected.

What do you say when you reach out to a potential role model? Let's start with the end game in mind. You might have visions of becoming best buddies who hang out on weekends and have a deep mutual respect for one another's life's work. Things could certainly end up there someday, but that's like thinking about marriage before you've even been on a first date! It's best to set realistic expectations and form an "ask" that's as easy as possible for the other person to deliver on.

You best option in virtually every situation is to ask for a short, targeted conversation about the person's experience or expertise. That's it. You don't ask for a job interview, an introduction to one of their contacts, or for any other favor. It's just not appropriate for someone you haven't met. Asking someone for a small amount of their time because you admire them and want to learn more about them is pretty close to universally flattering. Most people love talking about themselves and do want to help others, and if they can find time in their schedule, they will be happy to help you.

If you're having a hard time picturing yourself out there like this, it helps to know how often people do it. I get messages from total strangers all the time who want to have a call with me or take me to coffee so they can learn more about my experience. This also happens with consistent regularity to my senior-level colleagues and friends. These messages are no big deal. If I think I can help someone, I'm happy to chat. I might not always be able to schedule a call within the next month, but if the person is patient, we can usually make it happen.

When I was writing this book, I interviewed people to help add more interesting and diverse perspectives, stories, and data. I had to take some of my own medicine here and reach out to strangers whose expertise I admire. I felt a little nervous about it in the beginning (I'm an introvert, after all!), but I reminded myself that the worst that could happen is that someone would say no. I thought about all the times I had been contacted by total strangers and the strategies that worked the best for piquing my interest. From there, I made a list of people I wanted to speak with and started reaching out. I wanted my role models to know a little about me, why I admired them, and what I was asking for in terms of next steps.

Here is a real email I sent to David Rosell, one of the people I contacted when writing this book:

Hi David,

I live in Tumalo and have read several of your books after seeing them on the bookstand at the Redmond Airport. I found them to be quite good, and even bought the Keep Climbing one for my 23-year-old son for his birthday this year (he likes learning about this stuff) ...

My question for you is whether you'd be willing to give me a small amount of time to contribute to a book I'm writing. The book is focused on living an inspired and fulfilling life, based in large part on my own life journey, being surrounded by a wide spectrum of individuals who've lived remarkable lives (astronauts, businesspeople, movie stars, professional athletes, and regular folks). One of the chapters in my book focuses on preserving financial flexibility to retain the ability to pursue inspiring and fulfilling paths in life, vs being constrained by too many financial burdens that people create for themselves.

Would you be willing to get together for 30–45 minutes and talk about this and provide feedback on this chapter in my book (plus any other areas that interest you)? I love your personal story around seal coating driveways, buying a used vs a new car, investing to create compelling travel experiences, etc., and I think those themes fit well with the overall messages in my book. Also, since you've written several books, I'd love to hear any additional advice on that front.

Here's my LinkedIn profile to give you a bit more background on me, and here's my contact information if you're willing to connect in person sometime.

Thanks in advance,
Darren Pleasance

As you can see, I hit on a few key elements in this outreach:

➢ **Research and preparation.** I gathered a decent amount of information about David before I contacted him. This not only helped me understand him better, but it also enabled me to tailor my message and show that I had done my homework. This research also became the basis for having a more meaningful conversation later.

➢ **Admiration.** I honestly do admire David (why else would I be reaching out to him?), so I wanted to ensure that it came across in my email. I didn't make it cheesy or over the top, and I alluded to how he has reached a level of success that I aspire to reach. (I would love to have my book available in airports—especially in my home airport in Bend, Oregon!)

➢ **Common ground.** In my email, I mentioned how David's expertise aligns with the kind of content I'm writing. This showed that I am interested in talking with him about topics he knows well and that we would likely have an easy conversation.

➢ **Brevity.** This email was on the longer side of what I'm used to sending, but I felt like I needed the space to hit on all my key points. I wouldn't recommend going much longer than this because lengthy messages are more difficult and time consuming for people to respond to—even when the message is nothing but praise. (When someone writes a long message, people feel like they need to respond with more than a few sentences. As a result, they procrastinate, and the chance of them never responding goes up dramatically.)

➢ **Follow up.** Perhaps a reflection of my last point, David did not initially respond. I got an "out of office" response when I first contacted him, so I knew he was busy. I sent a follow-up email 12 days later:

Hi David,

I know you were traveling when I sent this originally so I'm resending it to see if we might find a time to connect in Bend.

I'd appreciate your input on the book I'm writing.

Thanks a lot.
Darren

David responded a few hours later! I'm glad I decided to check in with him, or it's possible my email could have become permanently buried in his inbox. We ended up meeting a couple weeks later, and we had an interesting conversation that was highly beneficial to my research for this project. I also enjoyed learning about David's experience becoming an author, since I was traveling down the same path.

Introducing yourself to strangers you admire can be a nerve-racking experience, but it's worth it. As long as you are polite and respectful of the person's time, you are likely to get a positive response. If someone is too busy to respond, or they turn you down, don't sweat it. There are plenty of other role-model fish in the sea, and taking the initiative to reach out can be a valuable experience in itself.

Additionally, many role models are likely to be people who've written books, or spoken at events such as TED, or have been interviewed about aspects of their lives. So even if you aren't successful in getting to speak to your role models in person, there are often ways to learn a lot about them and their own life journeys through these other means. For me, individuals such as Richard Branson, Elon Musk, Oprah Winfrey, and Brene Brown, and such lesser-known folks as Alaska bush pilot Don Sheldon, were all able to influence my path in life, even though I've never actually met them, by simply reading their books, watching them speak on YouTube, or listening to them being interviewed by other people. For someone to become a role model and to convey wisdom and learning, they don't actually have to meet you, though moving on to becoming a mentor or a sponsor does require actual live interactions with each other.

As you think about the path toward your true north, people are undoubtedly a key element. From best friends to colleagues to mentors, relationships have a way of shaping both your day-to-day experience and your life's course. That's why it's so important to surround yourself with individuals who inspire you, support you, and challenge you to grow. When you have the right people in your life, so much more is possible.

While you're working on strengthening your own relationships, don't forget to pay it forward and seek out opportunities to help other people expand their networks of relationships. As you start to make connections with individuals who inspire you, you'll likely find opportunities to connect people who wouldn't otherwise know each other. The act of connecting people is a great way to strengthen the community of people you have in your life. It also amplifies your efforts, since those individuals who benefit from your introductions will very often reciprocate by proactively introducing you to people you hadn't even thought of trying to meet. It becomes a virtuous cycle with your network of relationships getting bigger and stronger over time. It's these relationships that almost universally become the foundation for the inspiring opportunities that come your way throughout your life.

CHAPTER 4

Become great at what you love

When Deke Sharon was a baby, his parents noticed his penchant for music before he could even speak. A good melody would catch his ear, and his face would light up when certain songs were played. He loved to bop around to a good beat, and family members got a kick out of his enthusiasm for the radio.

When Deke was five, his parents were looking for an activity for him to do outside of school, and they suggested either Mandarin Chinese lessons or joining a boys' choir. Deke jumped at the chance to join the choir. It wasn't long before it was obvious that Deke's musical talents put him on another level. He started performing professionally when he was eight, and his talent afforded him the opportunity to sing in operas across North America with the likes of Luciano Pavarotti.

Though having that level of success at such a young age is impressive to adults, Deke's elementary-school peers didn't exactly consider opera to be cool, so his experiences didn't give him much cache on the playground. If anything, it made it harder for Deke to fit in. He felt the pressure of wanting to be like everyone else, but the problem was that he didn't have the same interests. He grappled with this for a while, wondering if he should find a new hobby that his classmates would admire, or downplay his passion for singing.

Deke kept up with his music classes and finally decided that he loved it too much to focus on anything else. Instead of trying to fit in with a group of non-musical kids, he formed bonds with peers who shared his passion. Deke had found his people—and they encouraged him, inspired him, and pushed him to get even better.

He continued this trajectory into college, when he felt his interests begin to niche down into a specific area of study: a cappella. He loved the sound of many different voices coming together to sing harmonies and create the sounds that would normally be played by instruments. (Today, a cappella is more widely known, but in the late '80s, it was hardly a blip on the contemporary music radar, despite the success of Bobby McFerrin's "Don't Worry; Be Happy.") For Deke, it became a near obsession. He loved singing harmonies with fellow musicians and figuring out how to arrange popular songs in a cappella versions. He founded the Contemporary A Cappella Society in college and built a deep network of likeminded musicians.

His hard work paid off. Today, Deke is widely considered the father of contemporary a cappella music. He's arranged more than 2,000 songs, written six books, and worked with countless music legends including Ray Charles, James Brown, and Crosby, Stills & Nash. He was the music director and arranger for the movie *Pitch Perfect*, and he's worked on numerous other movies and TV shows over the years. Deke's level of expertise has allowed him to shape an inspired life doing what he loves.

We can all take a page out of Deke's book when it comes to greatness.

When you become great at something, the world is your oyster. Doors you didn't even know existed begin to open. You find yourself

Deke Sharon discovered early in his life that he loved music and used that passion to transform the world of a cappella forever.

connecting with interesting people who value your expertise and want to help you reach your goals. Opportunities crop up out of nowhere, and you're presented with choices that can have a positive impact on your life.

That's why greatness is something everyone should aspire to achieve in some area of their life. You don't have to be the very best in the world, but a good goal is to find a niche where you can be noticeably better than most. That will enable you to stand out for the skills and talent you've developed.

Enhancing strengths versus fixing weaknesses

The most natural path to become great at something is the one on which you're amplifying areas of strength that come most naturally to you. Research from the likes of Tom Rath, the author of *Strengths Finders*, has shown that the returns people get by nurturing and investing in a strength is far greater than the returns they get by trying to substantially change or improve weaker skills.

Unfortunately, this research does not typically align with what actually happens in most of the arenas where people get feedback on their performance, such as school, sports, and businesses. Most often, those feedback discussions focus on all the areas where people are underperforming relative to their peers. In other words, if you're excelling at something, you're likely to get a pat on the back from your teacher, coach, parents, or boss and then told to focus on something else. Instead of acknowledging that certain skills are weaknesses, these days, they're more often called "opportunities for improvement." This shows the pervasive mentality that no one should settle for being below average in anything. Not only is this unrealistic, but it takes the focus away from exploring how to capitalize more effectively on the areas where people show differential signs of energy and potential.

Don't get me wrong: this kind of feedback doesn't come from a bad place. It's simply given by people who are focusing on the tasks at hand, rather than the person who is completing the tasks. As a result, we very often get advice on how to "fix things" about ourselves that ultimately have very little to do with putting us on a path to living the life we want to live.

This is important to keep in mind whenever you get feedback on your performance. Ask yourself how the suggested improvements would help you on your own unique journey to greatness. If improving certain weakness would close some important gaps, then go all in. But if doing certain tasks better wouldn't necessarily help you, then it's time to examine whether the role or activity is the right fit in general.

Management consulting is an industry in which "extreme feedback" is the norm. Almost daily, managers provide feedback on ways to do things differently and better. As a result, consultants' growth and development trajectory is often outstanding, but at any point in time, all the areas where they are not performing up to expectations, or where skill gaps are preventing their continued career growth, become abundantly clear. At McKinsey, we called this "up or out." Consultants either continued to develop, shoring up their weaknesses enough to make it "up" to the next level, or they were "counseled out" to pursue a career outside McKinsey. (Though this may sound harsh, it was actually done in a very caring way that made the experience fully worthwhile regardless of whether team members continued "up" for many years or eventually found themselves "out" along the way.) What this approach optimized for was creating very good—and largely homogenous—consultants who all had a fairly universal and valuable set of "consulting skills."

This approach also put a spotlight on the fact that not everyone is destined to become a great consultant, no matter the fact that everyone joining McKinsey was extremely talented and accomplished when they entered. For those who ended up on the "out" path, it was most often because the skills that made them distinctive weren't necessarily the ones most required to be a great consultant, and a lot of the feedback along the way would begin to expose this mismatch. When the hard conversations would occur about a person needing to leave, it was always through the lens of helping that person land in a role in which their strengths were far more applicable to professional and personal success.

We often talked about everyone at McKinsey being an athlete, but many were playing the wrong sport. Think about Michael Jordan playing baseball. He was an OK baseball player, and certainly far better than I would ever be, but he was not great like he was when he played basketball. For each of us, much like with Michael Jordan, there's huge power in understanding where you have differential strengths relative to others and then leaning into that and playing the "sport" in which those skills set you apart the most.

Put in the time

Innate talent is definitely a factor when it comes to achieving greatness, but it will only get you so far. To truly become a master of your craft, you have to put in the time. That's why it's crucial to home in on what you love. When you enjoy something, you want to spend time doing it. Whether it's singing, playing soccer, or tinkering around under the hood of a car, it feels like fun instead of work. It has your full attention, and you seek out ways to learn more and deepen your skills and knowledge. This is critical for developing greatness because the real difference maker in mastery is time on task.

You might be familiar with the book *Outliers* by Malcolm Gladwell, where he writes about how it takes 10,000 hours of dedicated and intentional practice to become an expert in a particular field or skill. The concept is based on the work of psychologist Anders Ericsson, who conducted research on the development of expertise in various fields. He found that individuals who invested about 10,000 hours of focused effort into a single skill or field were able to reach a higher level of success than their peers.[3]

If 10,000 hours sounds like a lot, that's because it is. You can break it down in countless ways, but nothing makes it sound like a particularly easy lift:

➤ 1 hour per day takes approximately 27 years to mastery

➤ 2 hours per day takes approximately 13.5 years to mastery

➤ 4 hours per day, 5 days per week takes approximately 10 years to mastery

➤ 8 hours per day, 5 days per week, takes approximately 5 years to mastery

Any way you slice it, you'll need to dedicate a significant portion of your life to a specific skill or field if you want to become great at it and differentially better than others. That's why you need to have a genuine love for whatever it is that you're pursuing. To get to 10,000 hours, you will have to choose again and again (and again!) to invest your time in that one particular area.

Deke instinctually knew this from a young age. He told me that he was willing to accept a lower grade in French class because being good at something he didn't like wasn't worth the cost in time that he otherwise could have been spending on strengthening his music-related pursuits. While his classmates worked hard to perform well in every subject, Deke decided to concentrate his efforts on what he cared most about and where he wanted to build the most expertise: music and musical theater. As his grade in French dipped lower and lower, he remained steadfast that it was all part of his plan to perform exceptionally well in the areas he was most passionate about.

"What was Bruno Mars's GPA?" he asked me with a smirk.

"Doesn't matter," I replied.[4]

I see a glimmer of what Deke was like in school, and I can only imagine how his parents and French teacher felt about his educational strategy. Though I won't necessarily condone the idea of purposefully getting a bad grade in school, I can't help but see the logic of spending the most time on the things in which you excel and want to have as a major part of your life story.

Profession vs. hobby

You might be thinking how amazing it would be if you could earn a bundle from doing something you love so much that it doesn't even feel like work, but the reality is that jobs command very different compensations. Is it worth it to pursue a skill or field of study if you think you're unlikely to translate your level of mastery into a decent job?

Yes. A thousand times yes!

It's hard to know where your level of mastery will take you. Of course, it's smart to consider how your skills could translate into a full-time job, but that's not the only thing you should focus on. Life is not one-dimensional. Inspired people have a range of interests they pursue not because they expect a profit but because it helps them cultivate a more meaningful existence. The reward is doing the thing itself and becoming better at it.

It's certainly nice when the time and effort you spend working toward greatness ultimately leads to something you can monetize. But it's important to realize that you can very likely make a living, and a life, out of virtually anything you become great at. (Yes, there are professional board-game testers, cupcake tasters, and people who write the clever notes inside fortune cookies.) The world is a big place, and there are countless jobs out there that you have never even heard of. Every industry has niche positions that leverage unique skill sets, and with exponential changes in technology, new roles are being created daily. There are examples of inspired people doing virtually anything you can imagine.

I bring this up because I want to dispel the myth that there are good and bad skills to develop. If you're interested in something, do yourself a favor and check it out. You never know how your skills and passions will evolve from there or the opportunities that might come your way, particularly if you end up being far better than average at whatever skill it is that you're building.

On the flip side, there are a variety of reasons why you might be better off leveraging your greatness as a hobby rather than as a profession. Some lines of work are much more competitive than others. Having jaw-dropping talent isn't necessarily enough to get a steady job as a professional singer, actor, or athlete. That said, there are hundreds of other jobs that relate to those roles in which you could leverage your greatness and stay in the industry—if being in the industry is where you get your energy. Being a backup singer to a lead singer won't pay as well as being the lead—but at least you're on the stage. And sometimes, there's a great deal of value just being "on the stage," whether that stage is an actual stage, a movie set, the pit lane for a car-racing team, or the receptionist's desk at a really cool company. Opportunities in areas you care about will often emerge, and your chances of getting those opportunities go way up if you're close to the action. Taking a position that is just in the realm of your dream job might not be exactly your highest aspiration, but it will be directionally aligned with your goal.

But if your interest doesn't lie in those other positions, you might be better off developing your greatness as a hobby. If you're so passionate about something that you can't picture a life without it, you shouldn't compromise. Invest the time it takes to make it part of your life. To be great at something, and to feel the inspiration that comes from that, doesn't require that this area of interest be a full-time job. Greatness isn't about identity or ego; it's about having time and energy to devote to what lights you up.

I always loved flying, and when I was able to become a professional pilot and fly as my full-time job in my 20s, I felt as though I'd reached the ultimate level of success. The adventures I had and the people I met had me waking up every day excited to go to work and become even better at what I loved doing.

However, after a decade or so of flying professionally, I saw how my day-to-day experience was different from when I was purely flying for fun. I enjoyed my job, but taking three-week trips to the Caribbean each month and sitting at random airports waiting for my clients to return wasn't giving me the same level of inspiration as it had earlier in my career. While I was coming to this realization, I was back in school getting my MBA, and I stumbled into the world of management consulting. I began to develop an interest in pursuing that path for a while. My childhood goal of becoming an airline pilot wasn't materializing due a variety of factors (airlines going bankrupt, an abundance of experienced furloughed pilots), so I began thinking about what it would be like to step into consulting and transition from being a professional pilot to flying just for fun. One of the benefits of the management-consulting industry is the generous compensation, which was especially appealing for me in this scenario because flying is a somewhat expensive hobby.

Ultimately, I decided to change careers when that great opportunity with ADL came my way, and I made the conscious choice to walk away from, or at least postpone for several years, a career as an airline pilot. The job I took was based in Boston, and I was able to find a local airport about 20 minutes outside the city where I could continue to "scratch my flying itch" on the weekends by just renting a plane and flying for fun—while also investing time to build a whole new set of capabilities in the consulting industry. This was truly a case of having my cake and eating it too, where I continued to build my flying strengths and expand opportunities in that domain while at the same time opening up entirely new paths in my life that would serve to create so many inspiring experiences over the years ahead.

As my story illustrates, it's normal for your interests and passions to shift and evolve over time. And chances are that you're not just developing greatness in a single area of your life—you're honing multiple capabilities. When something lights you up, lean into it! Having numerous interests and talents will do nothing but add richness to your life and open the door for more opportunities down the road.

Know when to pivot

Living an inspired life looks different to everyone. Though there isn't one right answer, there is a wrong answer: following a path to greatness that you are not at all passionate about. That is a surefire recipe for feeling unfulfilled. Many people find themselves in this situation when they have been pressured into developing a skill set that doesn't light them up. Maybe their parents wanted them to become a doctor or lawyer, so they followed one of those "true north" career trajectories only to realize that although they're earning a generous salary and have a title that some people find impressive, they aren't happy. For others, maybe they felt pressured into developing a certain skill set because they demonstrated strong natural talents early on, and people thought it would be a shame for them to "waste" those talents—even if it meant doing something they don't enjoy. As a result, they fall into the trap of chasing achievement or wealth at the cost of happiness. In other cases, people simply find that their passions have evolved over time. Sometimes that spark of interest dies down or goes out completely. This is a confusing place to be, especially for those who have always had a clear vision of what they wanted in the future.

Whatever the cause for misalignment between passions and mastery, it's never too late to pivot. Here's where self-awareness, honesty, and bravery come into play. Your unique path to mastery isn't going to look like everyone else's. (That's a good thing, as we can't all be experts in the same area!) It can feel uncomfortable to truly lean into something you're passionate about. You might also feel vulnerable going after something that lights you up in a way other people can't relate to. But that's the beauty of discovering your greatness: it's all about authenticity.

It might seem like a lot of pressure to figure out exactly what you want to invest your time in, but the good news is that you don't have to decide now and be committed to it for the rest of your life. Part of being authentic is not always having everything figured out. You can explore different options, dabble in a variety of interests, and discover what sticks. The important thing is that you continue checking in with yourself to make sure you continue to enjoy what you're pursuing. If you need to adjust course, it's best to do so quickly rather than going down the same path simply out of habit.

It's also important to note that skills are often more transferable than people think. For example, you might invest a significant amount of time and energy into starting and growing a new business. You spend a few years of your life learning how to do everything from hiring to bookkeeping to managing inventory and posting ads on social media. Maybe you enjoy it for a while but ultimately decide that entrepreneurship is not for you. If you no longer want to run your own business, it's not like you've wasted those years of your life. You've developed many valuable skills that can be applied in a wide range of contexts, which will give you a head start in another direction.

This is encouraging if you think you might be approaching a fork in the road and don't know which way to go. Sometimes people think it's easiest to continue down the same path, especially after investing so much time in mastering something. But when it comes to living an inspired life, fear of change is not your friend. It's natural for interests and passions to evolve over time, and it's easier to stomach a change in direction if you recognize that you aren't starting at ground zero.

Strategies for building skills

Start broad: You might have the urge to start with a narrow definition of the skill you are pursuing, but try not to jump to that point too quickly. In the beginning, it's more about trying to find a "domain" that could be the foundation of the skills you build. Early on, I discovered that I loved flying and immediately zeroed in on being an airline pilot. Being young and inexperienced in the industry, it seemed like the natural trajectory—and the only one worth considering. However, looking back on this, it was clear that I'd defined the aviation space far too narrowly. I've come to discover that the world of aviation has so many paths within it, including not only being an airline pilot but also in such professions as bush pilot, corporate pilot, flight instructor, airshow performer, medivac pilot, military pilot, powerline patrol, aircraft mechanic, air-traffic controller, and many other aviation-related professions. For any skill you become great at, you'll discover a whole domain of opportunities in front of you that provide viable paths to living an inspired and fulfilling life.

Craft a unique niche: It's amazing how a combination of skills can come together and create something that is far more valuable than the sum of its part. This is how people differentiate their greatness and carve out a niche that is unique and marketable. Chris Burkard is a professional photographer and an excellent surfer. He decided to bring these two passions and skill sets together to specialize in taking pictures of surfers. There aren't many people in the world who can ride a wave while taking a beautiful shot, and Chris stands out as one of the best.

Leverage free resources: You can learn just about anything for free so long as you can invest the time. From books to YouTube to TED Talks and social media, we're living in an age when there is a wealth of content at our fingertips. My son, for example, built a great business when he was in high school by becoming really good at shooting and editing short videos. It started with him wanting to create short "edits" of himself skiing with his friends. This forced him to go online and learn how to film using his GoPro and then create videos with Apple's iMovie. He soon learned of the limitations of these tools and started watching YouTube videos on how to use Adobe Illustrator and similar editing applications while also learning about the wide range of cameras used to make great videos with more than just a GoPro. This allowed him to create more elegant and creative videos. A local business that saw one of his videos he posted online asked him to create a video for their company. This quickly snowballed in ways none of us predicted. By the time he headed to college, he had several tens of thousands of dollars in his bank account from local video jobs, was well connected to other videographers in the area, and was forming the foundation of what would become a major part of his life after college. All this success stemmed from him leaning into an area of interest and leveraging free resources to improve his skills.

Education: Formal education, such as a BA or MBA, can be a smart investment. But don't underestimate other options such as a trade school or community-college courses. Companies are increasingly looking for individuals with the right experience and skill sets, regardless of whether they went to college. In certain industries, the value of a college degree plays no role in whether a person gets the job. For some professions, such as being a doctor, of course college is a must. But for so many others, particularly a number of the digital jobs popping up these days, there are other educational routes that can be equally or more appropriate. The key is to pursue an educational path that is aligned with the life experience you want to pursue. Do not be swayed by all the opinions and judgment you may get from others around you.

Don't wait! When you're interested in something but hold off pursuing it, you're burning daylight. Developing skills takes time, and younger people tend to have more free time than those who are in their 30s and 40s when jobs become more demanding and kids enter the picture. The sooner you can get started, the quicker you'll gain momentum. And, like many things in life, there's never a "right time." You'll always be too busy, have too many other commitments, be too tired, or not have enough money. These are all the stories you will tell yourself as to why it doesn't make sense to pursue something that lights you up and is something that could be a major contributor to living a life well lived. As Nike says, "Just do it"—and take the first step. Even if it's small, just start, and then take another step and keep going. Slowly spend more time on this new thing while actively shifting time away from things that aren't aligned with the new future you want to create.

On-the-job experience: Nothing beats being onsite and in person and seeing firsthand how a job is actually performed. There are many ways to gain experience and build expertise that don't cost a lot of money. There are often internships, apprenticeships, or entry-level jobs that you could do on the side to start building skills in an area of interest. Although these paths might not pay well (or at all), they can provide invaluable information that either reinforces your desired trajectory or quickly shows you that you want to go a different direction. In either case, you will also gain value from building a network of relationships that may eventually be sources of more substantial opportunities in your areas of interest.

But what if I don't really know what I would love to do?

This question comes up a lot when I talk to people about discovering their true north and building an inspired and fulfilling life. I started these talks with parents of middle-school and high-school students, an age when having a level of ambiguity about "what you want to be when you grow up" is quite natural. Upon conducting further research, I found that this same level of ambiguity often resides in people well into their working years—and sometimes well into their retirement years. The question is an important one, and it applies universally to just about everyone.

It is essential to put the work into uncovering what drives you and knowing where your passions lie. At the core of this journey resides the need for true and deep introspection about what really *matters* to you. There are many great books on this topic, and I recommend *What Motivates Me* and *The Passion Test*. Both books provide a set of frameworks and exercises for discovering the types of activities that will more naturally light you up and give you energy to pursue something with vigor in ways that perhaps don't exist in your current life. If you feel a need for more guidance on uncovering passions, both books are a good start. In the meantime, here are a few questions to consider:

➢ What do you want to be known for?

➢ What experiences would you love to have be part of your story when you're looking back on your life many years from now?

➢ What changes would you like to affect in the world if you could?

➢ Who are the types of people you most admire, and what is it about them that you admire?

➤ What paths in life did you not take because someone earlier in your life said no or talked you out of it?

➤ How do you choose to spend your free time, and where do you naturally procrastinate? (What magazines do you pick up when you have a free moment? What YouTube videos do you find yourself wanting to watch the most? Who are the people you like to read about or listen to? What is it about them that intrigues you?)

These are all important questions to ponder because at the root of each of them is a signal around what it is that will light you up and open the doors to an inspired and fulfilling life.

Thinking back to my childhood, the answers to many of these questions pointed to aviation. I discovered airplanes purely by accident as a kid driving by a local park and seeing an elderly man flying a radio-controlled model plane with his nephew. I wanted to stop and watch, and fortunately, my mom was willing to do that. We parked the car and observed from a distance. The man eventually saw us and invited us over to see the plane up close. This began the start of a 40-year relationship in which I'd go to his house virtually every day after school to build model planes and learn from him. This blossomed into an interest in full-size aircraft that would have me riding my bike 30 minutes every day after school to the local airport to watch planes land and listen to the "pilot talk" on the radio. This led me to volunteering to help wash airplanes in exchange for free rides. For anyone paying attention, it was pretty clear where I was naturally gravitating toward spending my time as the emergence of this aviation passion was cultivated and ultimately flourished. Fortunately, I had parents who stepped back and allowed me to lean into something that was giving me so much energy. They didn't provide me with money, but they did give me encouragement and support as I was discovering my true north.

It's these types of scenarios that all of us should be watching for as we work to support each other in finding that passion that lights us up and gives us the energy to become great at something we care about.

Be true to yourself

There is often a great deal of fear and anxiety around pursuing a passion and aligning greatness with something that will ultimately pay the bills. People think they are being smart and doing their future self a favor by prioritizing earning potential or quick-hit personal gratification, but as we've established, money does not buy happiness. In fact, spending thousands of hours doing something you hate is a surefire way to live an uninspired life—no matter how much money you have in the bank.

When it comes to developing greatness, you have to be true to yourself. Invest in the activities that bring you energy. Hone your skills doing things that bring you joy. And don't forget to let go of other pursuits that are taking your time and energy and not delivering a return on investment. This is how you will shape and develop the skill sets that serve as the foundation for an inspired life.

CHAPTER 5

Financial flexibility

"Joseph Heller, an important and funny writer, and I were at a party given by a billionaire on Shelter Island. I said, 'Joe, how does it make you feel to know that our host only yesterday may have made more money than your novel Catch-22 has earned in its entire history?'

And Joe said, 'I've got something he can never have.'

And I said, 'What on Earth could that be, Joe?'

And Joe said, 'The knowledge that I've got enough.'"

— Kurt Vonnegut[5]

Wealth is usually thought about in the context of having more: a larger house, a luxury car, a closet full of sneakers. But the tricky thing about being wealthy is that it's often a moving target. When you earn more money, you tend to buy more, and that becomes the new normal. From there, it can turn into a vicious a cycle of earning, buying, wanting, and never feeling like you've fully arrived.

Research clearly shows that wealth does not buy happiness. Several studies reveal that money can boost happiness to a point, but it's less than most people would think. A well-known study from 2010 puts that point at a salary of $70,000 a year. More recent studies suggest that the number is closer to $100,000, which likely factors in inflation and other changes in the economy.[6] Although the exact numbers differ, researchers agree that any income beyond that point doesn't have much of a correlation to emotional well-being. These figures are certainly higher than the average American salary of $65,575, but they are a far stretch from being in the 1%.[7]

What does this tell us? People find happiness in living a comfortable life. Although that inherently means different things to different people, it shows us that more is not always better. The key thing to understand is that wealth for wealth's sake is *not* the key to living an inspired life. In fact, chasing wealth is a fool's errand. Instead of focusing on having more, it's better to realize when you have enough.

With wealth comes complexity, obligations, and, if not managed well, a set of "golden handcuffs" that constrain rather than expand your path in life. That's because when you purchase something, there is always a trade-off. Money goes out of your bank account and you get something in return. Smaller purchases are usually a simple one-time transaction, but larger ones are often paid for over time. So instead of making a quick exchange, you commit to a repeated, long-term trade-off: a 30-year mortgage, a car note, paying off the credit card you used to finance that overseas vacation. Making such decisions locks in your money today and in the future. The more funds you have allocated to expenses, the less flexibility you have to use them other ways. So even though you may have a large paycheck coming in, by the time you pay all your expenses and debts, there might not be anything left to put in the bank. That's how people often find themselves constrained by golden handcuffs that are keeping them stuck in a job they hate but can't quit because they need that income to pay their bills.

You don't want to get yourself in a spot where you don't have the freedom to make important choices that affect your quality of life and mental health. That kind of sacrifice is far greater than forgoing some of the nicer things you might want to buy. It can be hard to see it in the moment, but living below your means is actually one of the smartest things you can do.

The key to living an inspired life is to manage wealth creation in a way that provides "flexibility" to choose what you want to do and allows you to make those choices without undue risk or burden to yourself and those you care about. This flexibility is derived not only from managing the balance of your income versus expenses but also from the nature of your financial obligations relative to your ability to pay for them over time. Taking on a long-term obligation, such as a home mortgage, can be fine provided it doesn't stretch your finances to the point that a minor hiccup could affect your ability to pay that mortgage and thus cause your whole world to come crashing down. This can be addressed by either choosing a home (and associated mortgage) that is well within your earning potential or making sure you have enough savings to cover you for 6–12 months so that if/when something unexpected happens, it doesn't completely turn your life upside down. Of course, doing both things (reasonable living expenses, healthy savings level) is the best option for maximizing the "flexibility" you need to be able to lean into the opportunities with the greatest potential to help you live an inspired life.

When you have a financial cushion, you can make decisions based on happiness. Although money doesn't actually buy happiness, it can certainly help get you out of a negative situation. If you find yourself in a job that makes you miserable, having a decent amount of savings affords you the option of quitting your job before finding a new one. The same mentality is true for relationships: you never want to feel like you have to stay in an unhealthy partnership because you are financially dependent. In many ways, money buys freedom of choice. If you're in a situation that is detrimental to your happiness or general well-being, a little savings can go a very long way.

Just as importantly, money can give you the flexibility to pursue your passions. You never know when the perfect moment is going to present itself to you. Maybe it's the opportunity to spend six months living abroad, start a business with your best friend, or accept your dream job (even if it, unfortunately, pays less than your current job). Maybe there's a family reunion at Disney World, your kid gets into their dream university, or you have the chance to spend time with a celebrity you deeply admire (as long as you can get yourself to London tomorrow!).

I can't tell you the number of individuals I've come across who've had opportunities to do amazing things in their lives but turned them down due to the perceived "risks" and having loaded up on debt and financial obligations such that those risks of pursuing those new opportunities were too high. If they'd had a large-enough monthly income to pay for all the expenses they'd taken on, or if they'd had a nice "safety cushion" in the bank to cover potential downsides, they could have easily chosen to take the more interesting and inspiring path that had emerged in front of them.

When you're working hard to follow your passions, become great at what you do, and build promising relationships, opportunities will crop up more often than you might anticipate. The value of freedom and flexibility truly cannot be overstated.

Personally, I made it a point to never have to say no to an opportunity as a result of getting myself so over my head in financial obligations that the risk of pursuing that opportunity was financially too high. When I left my flying job in my late 20s to get my MBA, I had been diligently putting money aside for multiple years. I didn't have an end game in mind for spending it, but I'd always valued freedom and autonomy and figured that having some savings could help support those values. When the opportunity to go to UCLA for two years presented itself, I was able to say yes and move to Los Angeles. (I chose UCLA in part because it was relatively close to Santa Barbara, where my job had been, which allowed me to work part time there when they needed me while also going to school full time. This enabled me to keep some money flowing in.) When I graduated from UCLA with my MBA, I was offered a job making twice what I had been making in my prior job, along with a very nice signing bonus that I immediately set aside and would eventually use for a down payment on my first house in Boston.

I had similar experiences when I left McKinsey to join Google. I actually took a pay cut when I made that change, and my regular compensation was replaced by a mix of cash and stock at Google. Fortunately, I had enough savings set aside so I knew that if the stock price didn't go up, or my bonuses weren't as large as I hoped they would be, I had the necessary financial cushion to weather it for a couple years. This knowledge gave me the comfort to say yes to Google when they offered me a job and enticed me to walk away from the great role I had been in at McKinsey for over 14 years. A similar scenario played out when I left Google six years later to join Cisco. I was taking on a higher level of risk with that new job, but I also had the backstop of savings to cover me in case things didn't go the way I'd hoped they would. This "backstop" of financial well-being provided me with the confidence and courage to take on new, exciting opportunities.

Taking money out of the career equation (even for a short period of time) is a liberating experience. I never wanted to turn down an opportunity or stay in a job purely because I needed the money. I always wanted to know in my mind that if my job went away tomorrow, I would be fine—at least for a while. This position enabled me to remain genuinely happy in all my roles, which I consistently stayed in for many years, because I knew I was there not because I had to but because I chose to. And when opportunities eventually came my way, I could evaluate them based on the merits of the opportunity itself and not through the lens of whether I could afford to take that risk. For me, being able to step into those moments was always a hallmark of living an inspired and fulfilling life.

Financial rules to live by

Creating the kind of financial flexibility that supports an inspired life requires intention and time. Maybe you're lucky enough to have a healthy trust fund that provides you with the financial cushion we're talking about here. But for most of us, we start out with little to nothing in the bank and spend our teens, 20s, and beyond just trying to keep up and put a few dollars away to buy something fun, or perhaps to save for a rainy day. That's all good, but it's the discipline, consistency, and choosing not to take on hefty financial obligations that ultimately expand the options you have in life. Small but important choices have a huge impact on how this journey plays out.

Financial strategies vary depending on your goals, age, and many other factors. But a handful of choices almost always hold true no matter your situation. You're probably familiar with most of these, but chances are you could be doing more to incorporate these strategies into your life on an ongoing basis.

> ➤ **Understand investments versus expenses.** This topic sounds fairly straightforward, but people get it mixed up all the time,

since investments and expenses both cost money. The key differentiator is that investments should pay off later. An education, though expensive, should be an investment. A fancy car, though fun, is almost always an expense because the value typically goes down over time. The more money you put into investments rather than expenses, the more you can expect to earn later as a return on those investments.

➤ **Consider how to save money on school.** Though an education is an investment, that doesn't mean you should dig yourself into overwhelming debt for it. There are many community colleges that offer an inexpensive two-year program that enables you to then transfer to a four-year college after that and graduate from a good school at about half the cost. This can save tens of thousands of dollars. My wife, Lisa, went this route, and it made a lot of sense for her and established a path down the road to a great graduate school from which she earned her master's in physical therapy.

➤ **Leverage the power of compounding.** If you save $5 per day, it'll add up to $150 per month. If you invest that and get a return of 5 percent over 20 years, you will have $61,655 instead of the $36,500 you invested.[8] Leveraging the power of compounding is a no-brainer, and the earlier you can start saving, the better. Set up an automatic withdrawal from your checking or savings account into an investment account, such as an IRA or a non-retirement mutual fund at a high-quality, low-cost firm such as Vanguard or Fidelity. This is how you pay yourself first. And if you have less success budgeting after this, at least you're still saving and creating the financial freedom to choose.

➤ **Spend money on things that bring you joy.** After you've planned for your fixed expenses (including putting money away for an emergency fund and retirement), hopefully you'll have a bit left over. Even if it only feels like pocket money, you should know that certain ways of spending it are inherently better than others. Pay attention to how you feel about what you buy—not the kick of adrenalin you get when you swipe your credit card but how you feel days, weeks, or months later. Certain purchases have a much greater impact on joy than others do. Experiences with friends and loved ones tend to have the biggest bang for the buck because such moments also create memories that can bring joy that lasts a lifetime. These experience also often help to strengthen relationships that could result in new opportunities coming your way in the future.

➤ **Pay off your most expensive debt first.** Credit cards usually have a higher interest rate than student loans, car loans, your mortgage, and just about everything else. It's best not to let expensive debt get too high in the first place because it can quickly get the best of you. Try to pay off your credit cards every month. Otherwise, you'll essentially just keep throwing money out the window.

➤ **Share expenses whenever you can.** I own half an airplane. That might sound silly, but it's true! I found someone to split the costs and usage with me, and it's been a huge win. Some things are easier to share than others, but don't be afraid to think outside the box. My friend arranged a nanny share with two of her neighbors who also had one child each such that they pay a nanny $25 an hour to watch all three kids. This breaks down to only $8.33 an hour per child. When the families switched from the local daycare center to the nanny share, it saved each family about $700 a month, which adds up to $8,400 a year.

➤ **Buy used.** You can save a bundle opting for gently used items instead of new. A used car is the best example, as cars lose thousands of dollars in value the second they leave the lot. Beyond that, you can find everything from furniture to appliances to fine China on places such as Facebook Marketplace, Craigslist, and a host of other online sites. Buying used is incredibly easy, and it's a good idea to invest those savings.

➤ **If you won't use it often, rent it instead of buying.** Sometimes it's appealing to own something that doesn't make financial sense to purchase. There are many things you can rent for a fraction of what you would pay to buy it (snowmobiles, power washers, etc.).

➤ **If your employer offers 401(k) matching, take advantage of it.** When your company is offering to give you extra money for free, you shouldn't turn it down. Though you might not be taking advantage of 401(k) matching because the money you'll earn doesn't feel real to you if you can't actually spend it for decades, trust me: if you commit to making those contributions, your future self will thank you.

➤ **Leverage rewards.** Many credits card offer good cash-back programs that are an easy way to get more money in your pocket without having to do anything extra.

➤ **Downsizing is positive.** The lower your expenses, the less you need to earn in order to have enough. That's why sometimes the easiest way to increase your cashflow is to decrease your monthly expenditures. If you're in over your head or starting to worry that your finances are heading in that direction, ask yourself if you REALLY need all the trappings of the life you've created. Do you need the size of house or apartment you have? Do you need the nice car you're driving? Do you need the golf club membership that extracts hundreds of dollars from your bank account every month? Maybe you do, but very often these are obligations that get created along your journey through life that get "locked in" and are seemingly unchangeable. Instead, perhaps downsizing to a more reasonable-sized dwelling, driving a less-fancy car, or making any number of other "compromises" would meet your needs equally well while helping you build the financial cushion. Instead of thinking about what you're getting rid of, focus on what you're gaining. Moving into a smaller home might not be ideal, but saving $1,000 a month could improve your lifestyle in myriad ways. Downsizing is a smart strategy for avoiding debt as well as pulling yourself out of it.

As a teenager, David Rosell, author of many financial well-being books including *Failure Is Not an Option: Creating Certainty in the Uncertainty of Retirement* and *Keep Climbing, A Millennial's Guide to Finance*, both of which exemplify these principles beautifully, learned about the power of compounding and "buying used" when his grandmother admonished him for seeking to buy an expensive new car. He had been saving for it for years, which he thought was a financially responsible thing to do. His grandmother disagreed. She told him that he should buy a nice used car instead and then take the money he had saved and open an IRA, in which his cash would grow tax-free in stocks for the decades ahead. She showed him how a small investment early in life can become a huge windfall down the road purely through the power of compounding. He followed his grandmother's advice, which ended up not only paying off in spades down the road but helped spark his interest in financial education and, ultimately, wealth management.

Today, David splits his time between Bend and Jackson, Wyoming. His partner is a woman he met on one of his "off-season" adventures around the world. His daughter opened her first Roth IRA at age 18 and attended university in New Zealand (she's a dual citizen thanks to her mother being from there), which provided her with an amazing life experience and led to her first job out of college working for a marketing firm in Australia. David also recently bought a very well maintained and barely used "previously owned" RV for about 10 percent the price of a new one, which is allowing him and his partner to add several new adventures and experiences in his "retirement years." By the way, David still works, but as he told me during our interview for this book, "I retired years ago when I realized that retirement simply means that I get to do every day exactly what I want to be doing—including doing the work with the clients I want to help—while enjoying the experiences I want to have."

For more examples and tips and tricks for systematically building financial flexibility and making smart financial choices, there are lots of great books on this topic—and I've personally found David Rosell's books to be both inspiring as well as highly practical and insightful. I also found enormous value in a book called *More Wealth without Risk* by Charles Givens. I read it in high school, and it helped me establish a strong foundational set of behaviors that benefit me to this day. I bought books from both of these authors for each of my children because the advice they convey is so foundational to living your best life.

David Rosell started making money by sealing driveways as a teenager;
his grandmother taught him the value of being frugal and of learning how to invest,
which provided him the flexibility to pursue the outdoor adventures he craved.

Avoid wealth traps

When I was a private jet pilot, I spent a great deal of time with ultra-wealthy individuals. I frequently accompanied my clients on their vacations, and I was always along for the whole ride since I needed to stay near the plane to fly them back home. I won't lie—it was a nice gig! One client in particular sticks out in my mind. I'd fly him down to the Caribbean, where he kept his yacht. He stayed on the boat the whole trip while I remained onshore at a local hotel. He would anchor the boat just offshore, and I would often swim out in the morning through the aquamarine water to have breakfast on board—and I was free to spend the day however I pleased. Usually, that meant lazing around in the sun and taking a dip whenever it got too hot. It was a dream for me and could hardly be counted as "work" once I landed the plane, since all that was required of me was my physical presence—in paradise no less.

My client, on the other hand, did not spend much of his time relaxing. Despite being in one of the most beautiful places in the world on a luxury yacht with hired hands, he often had his head down, working. As far as he was concerned, his business responsibilities didn't stop when he was on vacation. To maintain that lifestyle, he couldn't take a break.

His wife and grown kids often flew out separately to join him, and it was easy to see that their family dynamic was troubled. They didn't spend much time together outside these vacations, and although they were physically together on the boat, my client was still working.

Healthy relationships take time, and that was the one thing he didn't have. He was so consumed with running his businesses and generating wealth that he made everything else in his life a lessor priority. Since he made money his primary focus, his wife and kids followed suit, and it became a vicious cycle. Conversations centered on what the family members wanted dad to buy them and what sorts of things their friends had recently bought, as well as infighting among family members over who had received more than another and how this wasn't "fair" with a corresponding demand for resolution.

I'd often also see situations where we'd meet up with friends of my client who were even wealthier and, although we'd arrive to a beautiful location in a private jet, one of the friends would inevitably arrive in a bigger jet and would get whisked away to their home via their private helicopter. My client would look wistfully at his friend and then complain to me that they had once been equally poor but the other guy had done so much better. This really drove home to me that there was no such thing as "enough" to him and he would forever be dissatisfied with everything he achieved.

I couldn't help but think how much better off they would all be if my client chose to sell his businesses and retire immediately to spend time with his family and enjoy the fruits of his labor and earned success. He was far beyond the point where earning more money was making him happier, and he had become consumed by the pursuit of "more." All other areas of his life were suffering as a result. Even though it looked like he had it made, he wasn't enjoying it.

More is not always more—even when it's fancy and shiny and would make all your social-media followers green with envy. Check your ego and beware of spending money in lavish ways that will not offer the return you expect. It's much better to actually be happy than to focus on keeping up with—or besting—the Joneses.

Managing your finances to support your true north doesn't mean you don't treat yourself to special things once in a while—and it doesn't mean you don't take trips or pursue interesting adventures. But it does mean you are thoughtful about how you do these things, make choices that give you the biggest bang for the buck, and then leverage the savings to create the flexibility over time to pursue the inevitable exciting opportunities when they emerge.

CHAPTER 6

Your 168 hours

Years ago, after I had recently joined McKinsey, I was starting to feel the burden of having too much to do and not enough time to accomplish it all. The management-consulting industry is notoriously demanding from a time standpoint, with people often working more than 12-hour days plus a few hours on the weekends and pulling periodic all-nighters, not to mention having to travel four days a week and living out of a suitcase. I noticed that after my colleagues had spent a year or two in this lifestyle, they'd complain about their work/life balance—or lack thereof—and then quit shortly thereafter. I didn't want that to happen to me.

I was attending a McKinsey training event a few years into my time at the company when I looked around the room and felt like I could see into the future; I knew who would still be at the company in a year and who would move on. It wasn't that hard to see given the number of my colleagues who were so visibly downtrodden. But what was perplexing to me was that while some of them were clearly struggling, others were doing just fine. In fact, a handful of people seemed to be fully energized by their experience working at the company. Why was the lifestyle sustainable for some individuals, whereas others were burned out and miserable?

After extensive reflection, I realized that most people were thinking about the idea of work/life balance as a function of time, which wasn't the right way to look at it. We all had the same 168 hours a week (24 hours x 7 days) to work with, and we were in a profession in which we were all over-indexed in terms of time at work. If time was the only metric, we were always going to come up short.

It also dawned on me that the concept of "balance" is a misnomer. Balance implies a level of equilibrium and steady state when in reality life is not static and "equilibrium" is at best a fleeting concept. Instead, the real question was around how we each choose to spend our 168 hours each week, which, by definition, also includes the choices we make about where NOT to spend our time.

Julie Morgenstern, a six-time best-selling author on time management and organization, reinforces in her book *Time Management from the Inside Out* that good time management is not about creating the perfectly balanced life in which everything always goes as expected. It's about having the tools to get back to center, and to stay true to your own goals when you get thrown off-track.

As I listened to stories of my colleagues, it was clear that many of them were choosing to spend their 168 hours each week on activities that were draining them of energy and adding enormous levels of stress. Conversely, other colleagues were clearly choosing to spend their time in more inspiring ways.

These were the colleagues who had fun stories every Monday morning about the interesting things they did over the weekend. They went to shows, concerts, and baseball games. They traveled (even though they had been traveling for work during the week). They had quirky hobbies such as swimming from Alcatraz to San Francisco, salsa dancing, motorcycle racing, or playing flamenco guitar. They talked about the fun things they did with family and silly moments they had hanging out with friends. Because their personal lives had such richness, every weekend left them feeling emotionally refreshed and recharged. They showed up at work on Monday as multifaceted human beings rather than management consultants who got to rest on the weekend.

Unfortunately, these individuals were in the minority. After taking the time to get to know many of my colleagues, I found that many of them didn't have much going on outside work. They spent most weekends at home relaxing, but they didn't seem to have rewarding personal lives that enabled them to feel joyful on a consistent basis. They rarely talked about doing anything special or fun, or spending quality time with loved ones. They didn't seem refreshed, happy, or even well rested on Mondays. Although they had just as much downtime as other colleagues did, it didn't feel like enough because that time wasn't well utilized. I understood how easily this could happen.

Working 60–80 hours per week has a way of eroding everything else outside of that. It's easy to get so tired that you forget to make plans with friends, pursue hobbies, or make the most of downtime. All that takes work, and when you're tired, work is the last thing you want to do. But the catch-22 is that it takes intentional effort to improve the way you spend your personal time.

Optimize for joy

When it comes to living an inspired life, the key premise for time management is simple: *spend more time doing things that bring you joy.*

It sounds obvious, but it's one of those things that is often easier said than done. From work to commuting to buying groceries and loading the dishwasher, sometimes the daily minutiae can become so all-encompassing that it's easy to lose sight of the fact that life should be enjoyable. Yes, *enjoyable.* I don't mean that in a "someday I'll have more time" kind of way. I mean it in a "here and now" kind of way. Life is a gift. And you never know how long that gift is going to last, and it would be a shame to hold off enjoying yourself until after it's too late.

The challenge lies in putting this concept into practice. It takes intentionality, but everyone can derive more happiness and satisfaction from their life by better managing their time. Some choices can make an immediate impact on the day-to-day, whereas others are part of a larger transformation.

You might think you have too many responsibilities and non-negotiables in your schedule to make a meaningful shift in the amount of time you can spend on activities that make you happy, but I bet you'd be surprised at how much time you can get back when you focus your efforts on what matters most to you.

Earlier in this book, you defined what an inspired life looks like to you. This chapter will help you dedicate more time to those priorities.

The time audit

If I have one superpower, it's my ability to bend time. It's funny because a bunch of my friends joke about how I have superhuman productivity, but my secret is that I am just incredibly aware of how long things actually take, and I'm intentional about how I spend my time.

Years ago, I started doing a time audit. I wanted to know where my 168 hours per week were going and whether I needed to make any changes to improve my quality of life. I began by mapping out what a perfect week would look like for me. I wanted to define it, see it on paper, and be able to compare it with my reality.

I didn't know it at the time, but this exercise would be life-changing. I was able to quickly identify gaps between my dream schedule and actual schedule and start making changes. I pinpointed the activities that were no longer serving me, the minor responsibilities that had become all-encompassing, and the daily routines that were eating up a shocking amount of time. From there, I was able to make room for the activities that truly mattered.

You've probably heard Peter Drucker's famous quote: "What gets measured gets managed."[9] With these wise words in mind, I'm going to lead you through creating your own dream week, as well as your time audit.

Let's start with your dream week. Though there are infinite ways of spending your time, I've found that just about everything boils down to five categories: wellness, career, chores, relationships, and "me time." You're likely to spend time on all these categories each week, although the amounts will fluctuate:

> **Wellness:** sleeping, eating, exercising, mediating, going to the doctor, etc.

> **Career:** working, attending conferences, traveling for work, commuting, etc.

> **Chores:** cooking, cleaning, running errands, personal grooming, daily minutiae, etc.

> **Relationships:** spending time with your kids, date nights, visiting your parents, talking to your best friend on the phone, going to your neighbor's birthday party, etc.

> **Me time:** hobbies, reading, listening to music, watching TV, recreational sports leagues, scrolling through social media, etc.

You might define some of these categories a bit differently than I would, and that's OK! Maybe cooking is more of a hobby than a chore, or your recreational soccer league is more about exercise than me time. You might also find that some activities fit under two categories evenly, and you experience a two-for-one impact, such as going out to dinner with your family. Whatever the case, think about how you would ideally want to spend your time and pick a primary category that makes the most sense for each activity.

When you're doing this exercise, it helps if you have an aspirational mindset that is rooted in reality. In other words, if you need to work full-time to earn a living, your schedule should include full-time hours in the career category. That way, you can work toward optimizing your time without making radical changes to your responsibilities right away. From there, if you want to make bigger changes, you can do so gradually.

Here's how my current dream schedule looks:

Darren's Ideal Week

100% = 168 Hours

Wellness (64)	Sleep (50)			Eating (10)	Exercise (4)
Career (60)	Travel (10)	Reviews (10)	Strategy (20)	Team (10)	Comms (10)
Chores (16)	Finances (1)	Housework (10)		Errands (5)	
Relationships (14)	Lisa (7)	Kids (2)	Relatives (1)	Friends (4)	
Me time (14)	Flying (5)	Social (6)	Reading / TV (3)		

This is the right structure for me, but your schedule might look totally different. Working 60 hours a week would feel like way too much to some people, but after years of holding time-intensive jobs, I know that as long as I'm at or under 60 hours a week, I'm OK. If you have young kids who live at home, you probably spend a lot more time with them than I currently spend with my grown kids who are out of the house.

Whatever makes sense for your current situation, write it down. Also know that this sort of schedule is simply an average and that every week will be a bit different. (I wrote down one hour to spend with extended family, thinking that there would be many weeks during which I wouldn't see them at all, and then we would spend most of the day together a few times a year.)

Your Ideal Week

100% = 168 Hours

Wellness (XX)	Sleep (XX)		Eating (XX)	Meditating (XX)	Exercising (XX)
Career (XX)	Focus 1 (XX)	Focus 2 (XX)	Focus 3 (XX)	Focus 4 (XX)	Focus 5 (XX)
Chores (XX)	Finances (XX)		Housework (XX)		Errands (XX)
Relationships (XX)	Spouse (XX)		Kids (XX)	Relatives (XX)	Friends (XX)
Me Time (XX)	Energizer 1 (XX)		Energizer 2 (XX)		Energizer 3 (XX)

Your next step is to do this exercise again, but this time recording how you actually spend your time. Take notes as you go about your day and stick with it every day for a whole week. At the end of the week, tally up your totals and fill in the chart.

Your Current Week

100% = 168 Hours

Wellness (XX)	Sleep (XX)		Eating (XX)	Meditating (XX)	Exercising (XX)
Career (XX)	Focus 1 (XX)	Focus 2 (XX)	Focus 3 (XX)	Focus 4 (XX)	Focus 5 (XX)
Chores (XX)	Finances (XX)		Housework (XX)		Errands (XX)
Relationships (XX)	Spouse (XX)		Kids (XX)	Relatives (XX)	Friends (XX)
Me Time (XX)	Energizer 1 (XX)		Energizer 2 (XX)		Energizer 3 (XX)

For an electronic version of the 168-hour chart,
use the QR code in the Introduction.

How does your dream week compare with your actual week?

The first time I did this exercise, I had some pretty big discrepancies. If you're finding the same thing, it just means you have a lot of opportunities to shape your schedule into one that better supports an inspired life.

Wellness

Let's start by discussing wellness, since the majority of our hours are typically spent here. Health is the foundation of life. When health is compromised, it impacts everything else. Despite this fact, sleep and exercise are often the first to be sidelined for other activities. It's OK to skip a workout here and there or lose a couple hours of sleep, but it doesn't take long for it to catch up with us.

When your body doesn't feel right, it affects every area of your life. You're more tired, stressed, and irritable, which makes it harder to do well at work, maintain positive relationships, and have the motivation to engage in activities you enjoy. When wellness starts to slip, you start down a slippery slope for every other category. I could go on about all the benefits of sleep and exercise, but there are plenty of other resources out there you can reference for that. Just know that when it comes to living an inspired life, the key is to not compromise wellness. Period.

Career

You might not have a ton of flexibility in your career category because you need to maintain a set schedule of working hours and hit certain goals. As you audit your time, it's interesting to see the total number of hours you spend working and also the subcategories that show what you do at work. You might find that you are spending significantly more time on low-value tasks than you realized, which is taking time away from responsibilities that should have a greater priority. (It's surprising how much five or 10 minutes here and there add up throughout the week!) Having awareness in where your time goes will help you become more intentional about focusing on the work that matters most and saving less-important tasks for later—if you get to them at all.

In addition to week-by-week fluctuations, it's important to understand that there are seasons in life. Sometimes work is much busier than usual, whether it's because you're on an especially demanding project, there's a client conference coming up, or there's extra work near quarter end. During these timeframes, you know that you'll need to put in more hours than usual. Though you may not love it, you've made a conscious decision to accept it as part of the job because it's temporary and worth it in the grand scheme of things. When you created your dream schedule, you probably didn't capture this point in time, so you might notice some major differences between your ideal week and your current week if you're going through a busy season. That's to be expected. Instead of lamenting your work/life balance during this season, acknowledge to yourself that it is the "heavy season" and focus on doing your role well, but also make a note that when the "season" is over (e.g., a major project is finished, a key deliverable is complete, a major milestone is met), you will make active choices to reset so that over the balance of the year, your mix of time looks like your ideal weekly chart. Make sure your heavy season doesn't become the new normal.

Chores

As you reflect on your audit, you might also find that chores are taking up more time than they need to and that you can get more efficient with how you go about doing them. You should certainly make an effort to drive change in those areas, since shifting a couple hours a week into other categories can make you feel noticeably different.

You should also recognize when time is more valuable than money. If you're spending an inordinate amount of time on chores, and that's cutting into other categories or adding stress at work, it might be time to stop doing some of those tasks. There are plenty of things you can hire someone else to do to free up your time and lower your stress. Spending a little money to gain hours back is often well worth it. There's an excellent book called *Buy Back Your Time* by Dan Martell that has helped me think differently about how I spend my time. His philosophy is that people should prioritize their time to do things that either give them energy or money (or both). Many of the tasks outside of that are prime for outsourcing. If you're starved for time because you're working so many hours, a great way to allocate some of your income could be to cut back on the responsibilities in your chores category.

Relationships

Numerous studies show how important it is to connect with other human beings. This includes family, friends, and community. We are social creatures (even the introverts!), and we do better when we aren't alone.

The good news for busy people is that when it comes to building and maintaining meaningful relationships, quality always trumps quantity. A great example of this is family time. There's a huge difference between everyone sitting in the same room staring at their phones and everyone sitting in the same room enjoying each other's company while being fully present engaging in a conversation or activity. Whenever possible, try to make the most of the time you have. This sounds like a simple concept, but it doesn't happen that often without being intentional. It's so easy to get distracted by our phones, the TV, or all the chores that need to get done around the house. Before we know it, the hour we had to catch up with family at the end of the day turns into maybe 10 minutes of quality time. In hindsight, that hour could have been better spent enjoying a nice walk, playing a game together, or going out for ice cream.

With this in mind, the challenge usually lies in planning. Think about the people you care about and figure out how to spend more quality time with them. Buy tickets to events happening four months from now. Plan a WebEx coffee catch-up with your college roommate. Ask your kids what they would want to do with you if they could pick anything. Hire a babysitter to come once a week so you can have a recurring date night with your partner. Put the effort in now so you can make the most of your time later. Trust me: it's worth it.

Me time

Not all downtime is created equal. Watching TV and zoning out is great in moderation, but you can do better with your me time. You've probably dabbled in a few hobbies over the years, such as team sports, cooking, or playing an instrument.

The older people get, the less time they tend to dedicate to the endeavors that are simply for entertainment. This is a shame, because many hobbies put us in "the zone," or what is often referred to as a state of "flow," which has a major impact on mental health. Popularized by psychologist and author Mihaly Csikszentmihalyi, flow is a mental state in which a person is fully immersed and focused on a task to the point where they lose track of time and their surroundings. Flow is characterized by a feeling of complete absorption, deep concentration, and enjoyment in the activity being performed. Csikszentmihalyi describes flow as "the state in which people are so involved in an activity that nothing else seems to matter; the experience itself is so enjoyable that people will do it even at great cost, for the sheer sake of doing it."

Spending time in a state of flow has a positive impact on mental health, happiness, and general life satisfaction. When you're in flow, you're living in the moment. Stress and anxiety wash away because you aren't worried about that assignment coming up next week or ruminating on that disagreement you had with your partner this morning. You're focused on the task at hand, which is something that brings you deep satisfaction and even joy.

If you think about some of your favorite activities and how you feel when you're doing them, you'll probably identify what puts you in a state of flow. It's usually activities that offer a good balance between challenge and skill. (If something is too easy, it will quickly get boring. If something is exceedingly difficult, it's too frustrating to be enjoyable.) Figuring out what puts you in a state of flow and prioritizing time for those activities is essential for living an inspired life.

For me, flying is the ultimate way to experience flow. When I'm up in the air piloting a plane, I love everything about it. From navigating the aircraft to contending with weather to communicating with air-traffic controllers, the experience is challenging enough to keep my full attention but not so difficult that it's stressful. It certainly wasn't quite like that in the beginning, though! Although I always loved flying, I had to reach a certain level of proficiency before I could relax and fully enjoy it. I'm so glad I stuck with flying and didn't give up when I experienced frustrations or setbacks because I now have a lifelong hobby that enriches my quality of life.

Is it difficult to find time to dedicate to flying? Absolutely! When I've had a 60-hour+ workweek, I'm tired, and I haven't spent much time with family or friends, sometimes I'm tempted to put flying on the back burner for a little while. If I absolutely must, I can go a couple weeks without flying, but it's only an option in extreme situations. Whenever I'm not flying on a regular basis, my quality of life goes down.

My lovely wife Lisa has always been incredibly supportive of my unwavering need to be in the air. She sees how I am a happier person when I dedicate hours to my hobby. It's one reason she doesn't complain when I've been away on business for a week and want to take my plane out almost as soon as I get home.

It helps that Lisa is passionate about a hobby as well. She has always loved horses, and we have a horse farm next to our house in Bend. Lisa loves taking care of her horses, spending time riding, and participating in horse shows. I see how it lights her up and enriches her life, and I know it's important to make sure she has enough time to dedicate to this love. For us, supporting one another in our hobbies has become a key tenet of our relationship.

As you think about changes that will support a transformation in how you spend your time, note that your career, wellness, and chores categories are important, but the real magic happens in the relationship and me-time categories. Thinking back to my colleagues who were experiencing burnout, I had a hunch that these were the areas they were neglecting. If you lose connection with the things that light you up, your mental health will suffer.

In your daily schedule, you can typically make room for these categories in the unstructured time before or after work and on the weekends. It's easy to underestimate these blocks of time. They're sprinkled throughout your week, and they often occur when you're tired, distracted, or transitioning from one thing to the next. Without proper planning and intentionality, people often let these hours pass without making the most of them. But this time is crucial for living an inspired life.

How to get time back

To dedicate more time to relationships and me time, you first need to free up some of your time that isn't being spent as well as it could be. Since the goal is to help you spend more time doing things that inspire you and make you feel fulfilled, let's go ahead and call out all the ways you can spend time that do not align with that goal:

> ➤ Spending time on things that you think you should do but don't enjoy

> ➤ Spending time on things that feed your ego or will lead other people to believe you are happy

> ➤ Piddling away time on unimportant and unrewarding tasks

> ➤ Reacting to others in the moment and spending time on what they want/need you to do

> ➤ Spending time maintaining the status quo and doing what you've always done

> ➤ Spending time trying to make as much money as possible

We all fall into these traps. In fact, it can be exceedingly difficult to stay out of them. But the people who live the most fulfilling lives find a way to protect their time and limit spending in these ways. As you go about your week and reflect on your time audit, think about how much of your day you could get back if you pulled back on the time sucks listed above. This is your low-hanging fruit.

Here are a few more tips to help you think about how you might be able to make meaningful shifts in your schedule:

Consider opportunity costs. When you choose to do something, you are saying no to doing something else. You might not mind agreeing to lead that school committee, but you need to recognize that it's a direct trade-off with something else from your me time/relationships categories. Look at your schedule and ask yourself what you can stop doing to make room for activities that would drive greater meaning in your life. And the next time someone asks you to do something that doesn't justify the opportunity cost, don't be afraid to turn them down. How you say no makes a huge difference in how the answer is perceived, and if you're strategic about it, you can still help others without investing a great deal of time. You might say something like, "I can't do exactly what you're asking, but I'd love to help you in another way." An excellent way to add value is to point them to a resource or introduce them to one of your contacts who might be a good person for them to know.

Ask for help. People often take on more than they need to—at work and at home. Think about the tasks you've proactively taken on that could be done by someone else. Sometimes this can actually help other people, especially if it's in the workplace, allowing others to step up and get more experience. You could have a colleague go to a meeting for you, with you helping to prep them, thus giving them exposure to new people and you getting that hour back to focus on something else of greater value to you.

Perfection is the enemy of progress. To live an inspired life, you need to get comfortable with not giving everything the same level of attention. People burn an incredible amount of time and energy going for "perfect" when "good" is enough to get the job done. This is especially true when it comes to your job, where there is pressure to perform. When I worked at McKinsey, we would create presentations that often had 60 or more slides in them, and my colleagues would often spend countless hours working on those decks. They regularly compromised their sleep, editing minute details into the wee hours of the morning. And you know what? Clients rarely noticed or appreciated the extreme effort that went into the details. All that mattered to them was a handful of slides that were the most important for the key messaging. Those few slides would get shown to the CEO or investors, so it was worth making them perfect, but the other slides only needed to be good. Realizing that early on at McKinsey helped me become efficient while also protecting my personal time.

Not everything will get done. We tend to think that everything will eventually get done when there's time. It won't. And that's OK! It's time to let go of the idea that we must complete all the projects we've ever considered doing, all the tasks other people have recommended we do, and whatever is left on the never-ending "nice to have" list. The reality is that some things are simply not worth the time. So drop the guilt about your lack of progress and permanently cross things off your list. This is how you will cut back on your chores category and make time for more important things. I use Google Keep to maintain a running list of to-dos that I'd like to get to eventually, but then every week I take a look at the list and make a conscious choice on which specific items I truly want to dedicate my time to that given week. There are certain items on my to-do list that are more than a year old. Again, that's OK. It just means that I've come across many other things that were fundamentally more important and made the call to focus on what matters most.

Not every email will get answered. This is an extension of the previous item but worth calling out individually. It's a fool's errand to try to answer every single email you receive. Many responses turn into a game of tennis, batting short replies back and forth, constantly feeding your inbox with new non-urgent messages and sucking your time and attention. Your best option is to set up good filters so that you don't miss emails from certain people (e.g., your boss) or that include important keywords. This will help you be more responsive where it matters so you can let the rest go. This will also help you prevent your professional life from consuming your personal life while still allowing you to be responsive to those who truly need your attention and making sure your time is well spent.

Get a two-for-one. Find quality ways to combine activities on your to-do list. This doesn't mean bringing your kids to work so they can play video games in the corner while you're on calls. Instead, try building a skill, such as working out, and doing it with a friend or your partner. Listen to a great audiobook while you do laundry so your chores feel more like me time. There are many ways to get a "two-fer," but you have to be intentional AND consciously make sure you maintain the "quality" aspect of that time so you're not just cramming two tasks together and then doing an average or worse job on each one.

Reassess your commute. If you commute to work, your career category takes up additional real estate on your schedule compared with a job that would allow you to work from home. You need to make sure it's worth it.

Whether driving or taking public transit to work, longer commute times are correlated with higher levels of stress and unhappiness. Understanding this research is vital in making better decisions around what jobs to take and where to live.

Most people grossly underestimate how much commute time impacts their quality of life. A team of researchers writing in the *Harvard Business Review* called this phenomenon the "commuter's bias." They conducted a study in which they asked more than 500 full-time U.S. employees from a wide range of industries to choose between two scenarios:

➢ Job 1: salary $67,000 a year; commuting time of 50 minutes each way

➢ Job 2: salary $64,000 a year; commuting time of 20 minutes each way

Participants were told that everything else in these scenarios would be equal, including advancement opportunities, how much they liked the job, and the quality of their neighborhood.

Which do you think people chose? And which would you select?

Eighty-four percent of people in the study chose Job 1, which would pay them an additional $3,000 per year but cost them an extra hour per workday. At 250 workdays per year, the extra $3,000 was essentially like earning $12/hour for the extra commute time, which was less than half their hourly rate at work. Researchers checked to confirm that participants could do this calculation, and they could; however, their responses reflected an inability to fully appreciate the psychological, emotional, and physical costs of longer travel times.[10]

Even if that extra $3,000 had a positive impact in certain ways, it would not come without a cost. A study of 26,000 employees conducted by the University of West England finds that every minute of commute time reduces both job and leisure satisfaction and also worsens mental health. Researchers concluded that adding 20 minutes to a daily commute has the same negative effect on job satisfaction as receiving a 19-percent pay cut. In another study, Harvard political scientist Robert Putnam found that for each extra 10-minute period people spent commuting, they had 10 percent fewer social connections, which led to greater isolation and unhappiness.[11]

Considering those two job options, it's easy to see how the lower-paying option is almost surely a much better choice when it comes to me time, relationships, and living an inspired life. Though no one can magically add more hours to their day, opting for a shorter commute has the same effect. Free time might not be priceless, but it's highly valuable. Make sure you aren't giving it away without careful consideration.

Beyond trying to eliminate or reduce your travel time, make the most of it. Get yourself into a positive headspace so you can relax and enjoy yourself as much as possible. Schedule catch-up calls with friends during long drives or listen to a good podcast or audiobook. And if you have the option to ride a bike or walk, take it, as doing so alleviates you from many of the negative effects associated with commute times spent in a car or on public transportation.

There's a reason why there are so many sayings about there not being enough hours in the day and time being our most precious commodity. We can't magically create more time or snap our fingers and become independently wealthy and no longer need to work. But what we can do is focus on quality over quantity when it comes to how we spend our precious free time.

Thinking back to my colleagues at McKinsey, I was able to pinpoint why certain ones remained happy and inspired while others struggled: what they did outside work mattered the most. Make sure you don't run out of time for the things that drive the greatest return on investment for your happiness and health. To stay on track for your true north, lean into the activities you enjoy and that give you energy.

CHAPTER 7

Staying the course

When Jim Wetherbee was 10 years old, like many kids his age, he wanted to become an astronaut. Outer space captivated him, and he wondered what it would be like to fly out beyond Earth's atmosphere. He knew there weren't many astronauts in the world and that it might be a long shot to become one of them, but he also was perhaps naïve enough at that time to set an audacious goal for himself and to start moving toward it. He thought about what would give him the best chance of becoming an astronaut, and he decided it made the most sense to start early. He considered himself to be an astronaut in training, so he began reading books about astronauts and learning what skill sets they possessed so that he could start leaning into those subjects. He knew that math and science would be important, and he pushed himself to excel in those areas. It helped that he was actually quite good at those subjects, such that he found that, although he was working on hard topics, he actually enjoyed the journey he was on. When it came time to apply for college, Jim chose to major in aeronautical engineering, as that was the path many astronauts had taken and it involved subject matter he was innately interested in. While in college, he discovered that many astronauts were also pilots and had become pilots through the armed services, so he decided to join the Navy.

Jim quickly realized that many pilots want to become astronauts—and that it's a highly competitive environment. But that did not deter him. He thought about what could give him the best advantages, and he landed on just being more prepared than most other people were. If he could learn more, practice more, and hone his skills more, if an opportunity came along to get to the next step in his journey to becoming an astronaut, he wanted to be better positioned than anyone else was likely to be. To this end, he began putting in extra time and effort whenever and wherever he could. When other pilots took a break to watch TV or hang out with their buddies, Jim used the flight simulator to practice, trying his hand at numerous flight scenarios over and over until the actions he would need to take became muscle memory. He also invested time to learn aircraft systems in more detail than virtually anyone else had so that if he were challenged with an emergency, his understanding of how things worked would allow him to troubleshoot a problem and find a potential solution far more rapidly, and effectively, than others could. As a result, he got so good at flying and managing potential emergencies that his skill level became a differentiator for him.

Jim also came to the realization that many people actively look for ways to avoid doing anything other than what they absolutely have to do. He was even given advice at one point to "never volunteer for anything" because doing so would just add more work to an already busy schedule. However, Jim had learned earlier in his life that volunteering for things often creates opportunities you might not anticipate and introduces you to people you wouldn't otherwise have the opportunity to get to know. He therefore adopted exactly the opposite mindset and said yes to every volunteer opportunity that came his way. In so doing, he established a reputation as a can-do person that his commanding officers would look to first whenever they needed something done or wanted to offer someone an opportunity.

As he kept flying for the Navy, people couldn't help but notice that he seemed destined for bigger things. In 1984, Jim was selected to join NASA's 10th group of astronauts. This was the beginning of a 21-year career as an astronaut, during which he flew six times on the space shuttle—including five times as commander. Jim says that he was able to have this level of success at NASA because of small, consistent actions that added up over time. He went well beyond what was required when it came to practicing a variety of emergency situations and, as a result, was the most prepared person for the job. All the time spent practicing his craft gave him a level of expertise that was hard to match. Jim was personifying the often-referenced quote "The harder I work, the luckier I get."

Commander Jim Wetherbee

Oftentimes when we hear about highly successful people reaching their ultimate dream, it's easy to think that they got there because of some superhuman talent. Although there are certain people who possess innate strengths that they are able to capitalize on to become great, there is almost always a massive amount of perseverance behind every person's journey to success. There were thousands—if not hundreds of thousands—of moments when they could have said, "Hey, I'm tired, and this isn't that fun anymore. I think I'll go do something else."

But they didn't. They worked hard to get what they wanted most, and finally, after countless small efforts that chipped away at that goal, their perseverance paid off.

When considering the essence of what it means to be fulfilled, a big part of it is feeling like you overcame challenges to reach your goal. Going through adversity makes you double down on your desire for the end state. You learn firsthand how much you want something because you discover how much you are willing to sacrifice for it. When you demonstrate perseverance and finally get what you've been working for, it's much more meaningful than if it were simply handed to you. It might seem like you wish you could snap your fingers and bridge the gap between where you are now and where you want to be, but if it were that easy, you wouldn't appreciate it in the same way or get that genuine feeling of fulfillment.

Another word that's often used in this context is "grit." In Angela Duckworth's book *Grit*, she defines it as perseverance combined with passion when working toward long-term goals. When you have grit, it's like the secret sauce that keeps you going when things get tough. You might experience setbacks, failures, or obstacles, but you're so passionate about your goal that you keep going.

I don't mean to sound like one of those motivational posters your high-school guidance counselor had hanging in their office, but perseverance really boils down to not quitting. I realize that such a "don't give up" message may feel overly simplistic, because when you're in a situation in which you're exhausted, frustrated, and want nothing more than to pack up and go home, the hardest thing in the entire world is to not give up! Knowing that you'll encounter plenty of moments like this throughout your life, I want to share some strategies for boosting perseverance when you need it the most. It won't always be easy, but I can tell you that it's well worth it!

Step into the role. An astronaut doesn't just wake up one day being an astronaut. They start becoming an astronaut from the moment they dream about it and then start making choices that move them closer to that outcome over time. Along the way, though they may not yet officially be an astronaut, they are 100 percent "being an astronaut" in everything they do. They are living authentically and courageously on their true-north path. Someday, they just might find themselves on a rocket into space, but if they don't, it doesn't take anything away from the fact that they were "being an astronaut" by doing all the things consistent with that for many years. When you have the courage to put all your energy into "being" what you want to become without insecurity, perseverance will feel easier. This mindset and behavior are not something you will regret, regardless of where it takes you.

Surround yourself with gritty people and stories. Having strong perseverance is both nature and nurture. Some people are born with a hunger or drive to keep going in certain areas (nature). But it's also a major help to be around others who demonstrate and celebrate perseverance (nurture). When you see other people getting knocked down but then getting back up, it shows you that it's normal; getting knocked down doesn't have to mean staying down. If you normalize what it feels like to get back up, it can become your automatic response.

Along this line, don't underestimate the power of immersing yourself in inspiring stories in which people show grit. You can do this through movies, books, TED Talks, or any other type of media. When you see the challenging circumstances that people have had to overcome in order to reach their goals, it can be both humbling and inspiring.

Embrace being an underdog. We all have our own disadvantages that make certain areas of life more difficult. This might be a physical disability, not having enough money to go to school or take lessons, or not having family support. Those kinds of circumstances can make a journey more difficult, but success can be even more rewarding.

Amelia Forczak, my editor for this book, has scotopic sensitivity syndrome, which causes symptoms similar to that of dyslexia. She distinctly remembers what it felt like to be the first person in her class to get knocked out of her 8th grade spelling bee. Despite not being a strong speller and sometimes writing letters and words backward, Amelia developed a love for writing. She kept a journal for years and dabbled in short stories, but she didn't like to show anyone her work because so much of the content was crossed out and rewritten. She decided to pursue writing as a career, even though it was a skill that didn't always come easily. After she graduated from journalism school, she was honing her craft writing blog posts, case studies, and white papers when she got the opportunity to ghostwrite a business book. The prospect of writing 65,000 words was scary, but she went for it anyway and didn't quit. The book ended up becoming a *New York Times* bestseller. Since then, she's written 13 more books and helped edit many others. Amelia knows firsthand how difficult it can be to get words on paper, so she finds a great deal of reward in helping other authors through the process.

Despite writing many successful books, she says it took her a long time to be open about having a condition that makes it harder for her to do her job. She thought clients would judge her or not want to work with her. But when she shared her story with a client for the first time, they pointed out that perseverance is a universally admirable quality, and people want to partner with those who are willing to work hard.

When you find yourself at a disadvantage in some way, don't automatically turn in a different direction. Figure out what you can do to embrace being the underdog. You might find added motivation to work harder and see what you can accomplish. This built-in grit will serve you well.

Track progress and celebrate small milestones. When you make tiny improvements over time, you sometimes lose sight of how much you've advanced. Try keeping a progress journal to both help you track your success and serve as a reminder that you should enjoy the journey. After all, it's not just about the big outcome you are trying to create for your life. There are numerous important milestones along the way. Feed your motivation by acknowledging your wins—however minor they might seem. Of course, you should celebrate positive outcomes, but you should also reward yourself when you put in hard work as part of the process. For example, if you're applying for jobs, don't just celebrate when you get a good offer; celebrate when you submit a certain number of applications! Acknowledging small victories also plays an important role in you recommitting to your journey.

Don't confuse setbacks with roadblocks. Depending on what your goals are, it's probably safe to say that at some point you will need to collaborate with others. This could be in school, at work, or through an association—and all these groups have rules, hierarchies, and systems for getting things done. As human beings, we are hardwired to have different relationships with rules and authority. Some people are natural rule followers who like to know what is expected from them in any situation so they can operate within that framework. Other people see rules and expectations as suggestions that could either help or hinder depending on the context. As you move forward in pursuit of your objective, it's helpful to have awareness in your relationship with rules and authority, as it will undoubtedly come into play in your journey when invariably someone will tell you that you can't do that thing you want to do.

Now, I want to be clear that I'm not suggesting that anyone break the law or do anything immoral or irresponsible. What I am saying is that there is often a fair amount of bureaucratic red tape across many companies, schools, institutions, associations, and governing bodies that can easily get in the way of progress. Sometimes these entities will say no to you and block you from whatever you are trying to accomplish. It can be difficult to understand the reasoning behind many of the policies and rules, and that reasoning can at times be flawed. Getting caught in this space can be incredibly frustrating. It might also seem like you've hit a roadblock (e.g., a person in a position of authority tells you directly that you can't move forward). But it's important to know that this is not always the case. Question the framework you're operating in and determine whether there's a way to turn a roadblock into just a setback.

Being involved in aviation for so many years, I've had a hand in plenty of airshows and aerobatic contests. To host the kind of event in which pilots do aerobatics, you need approval from the Federal Aviation Administration (FAA). Trust me: this is not always that easy to get, as there are many regulations in place about how airspace can be used, and the FAA is known at times for being incredibly bureaucratic. The first time I submitted an airspace-usage application to the FAA, it was denied without much of an explanation. But instead of simply taking no for an answer, I did some research to understand why my request had not been approved given that, from my perspective, my requests were within the guidelines of the regulations. As a follow-up, shortly after my first "denial," I got a little more information, asked the FAA representative some questions, altered my request, and submitted again. Yet I was turned down again.

The process went on like this maybe five more times. Most people in my position would have given up (and I'm sure the FAA rep thought to himself, "This guy again?!" each time I kept coming back). But I was convinced that what I was asking for was entirely within the guidelines of the rules we were working with, and that the primary reason for being turned down was not based on the merits of my request but rather on the fact that saying yes to me required the FAA representative to do a bit of extra work and take some extra personal risk by confirming that my requests were within the boundaries of the regulatory guidelines.

Finally, I was able to address all the FAA's safety and compliance concerns, and they approved my application to host the airshow. In the end, I had used my interactions with them to truly listen to what their concerns were and find ways to come back to reframe my asks in ways that were as aligned as possible with the goals and pressures that the FAA person was trying to navigate. After I was finally able to frame my asks through the lens of "improving safety" and aligning with the FAA's mission of promoting aviation—and I was able to demonstrate that I had no intention of giving up—I was able to achieve the outcome I'd been going after. Yes, I had to make concessions on my end to get approval, and we had to do things a bit differently than we initially planned, but that was OK.

Ultimately, this strategy paid off for me again later when I was selected for the role of western regional airspace liaison to the FAA because of my history of being able to partner with them to get things done. During my time in this role, I was able to accomplish significantly more than expected.

As I reflect on this, the only real difference I brought to the table was persistence and a willingness to try different approaches to ensure that I found a way to keep moving forward. Whenever the FAA said no to most other people once, twice, or even five times, they would just drop it. However, I kept going to figure out what I could do to make the request more amenable to them so they could approve it. I did that in large part because I simply don't believe that most roadblocks actually exist. There are almost always alternative solutions for getting around issues. Yes, there are certainly setbacks—but usually not roadblocks that stop progress dead in its tracks.

With that in mind, the next time someone says that what you are trying to do is impossible, instead of taking no for an answer, consider what could happen if you demonstrated creativity and persistence. You could also try pushing things a bit further than your comfort zone typically allows. You might not be able to move forward exactly the way you have in mind, but you could still make valuable progress down a slightly different path.

In any long and difficult process, there are plenty of times when throwing in the towel sounds pretty good. And in many cases, people do. They get frustrated, they lose interest, or they stop believing in their ability to achieve their desired outcome.

We've all been there. Every single one of us knows exactly what it feels like to want to quit. And in some cases, maybe we should. Maybe we've been working on something that seemed like it would give us energy and fulfillment only to learn that it doesn't. Or what we signed up for and what we're experiencing don't seem to align very well. But the problem with quitting is that people often do it too early before they've really had a chance to figure out whether what they are doing is worth the effort. When we quit early, we don't give ourselves a chance to see what we are fully capable of. And most of the time, we are capable of so much more than we realize.

Success doesn't have to happen overnight—and chances are that it won't. As long as you're making forward progress, you will get there eventually. Climbing any mountain takes one step at a time. You may want to be on the top of that mountain right at this very moment, but there's no better way to get there than to just keep taking one step forward at a time until you reach your goal. Patience is key for persistence, because sometimes it takes many years to reach the summit.

CHAPTER 8

Courage to choose

Courage is not the absence of fear but rather the fortitude to move forward in the face of that fear.

We've all witnessed courageous acts: stone-faced soldiers shipping off to war, firefighters rushing into the Twin Towers on 9/11, a kid on the playground standing up to a bully. These stunning acts of bravery leave us feeling deeply humbled. They make us wonder if these people are wired differently. *Maybe they don't experience fear!*

But that's impossible. Everyone feels afraid—even downright terrified—at times. It's part of our biology, passed down through genetics over thousands of years to help keep us alive. But along with a healthy sense of fear, we've developed the reasoning capabilities to evaluate our fears and choose how to move forward.

At its core, courage demands a conscious evaluation of priorities, goals, and personal convictions to determine whether they carry greater significance than succumbing to fear. It requires individuals to look beyond their immediate apprehensions and consider the potential consequences of their actions or inactions. As an example, firefighters may experience intense fear rushing into a burning building, but their focus shifts to a higher purpose that compels them to act despite feeling afraid. They make the conscious choice to overcome their emotions in the moment and do what they set out to do.

First responders and the military are often who people think of when it comes to acting courageously, but you don't have to be in a life-or-death situation to demonstrate courage. You tap into it every time you push past adversity in the hopes of driving better outcomes—for yourself or others. This can mean standing up against societal injustices, even when faced with opposition and potential harm; challenging the status quo instead of automatically following the herd; or showing vulnerability and embracing your true self, despite the fear of rejection or judgment.

Acting courageously means looking beyond your immediate circumstances and considering the potential long-term impact of your choices. In doing so, you recognize that personal growth, well-being, and a shot at something better outweigh the momentary discomfort or anxiety that fear brings.

Three areas to focus on

When it comes to living an inspired life, it's important to address courage head on, because we all need it to reach our goals. There are three key areas that tend to require an extra dose of courage.

Overcome inertia

As humans, we are creatures of habit. We take great comfort falling into routines, whether it's driving the same route to work, sitting in the same spot on the couch, or going back to the same restaurant (and ordering the same delicious sandwich!). When we find something that works for us, it feels good to keep doing it. Sure, we could try mixing it up, but that might make for a subpar experience. As the saying goes, *if it ain't broke, don't fix it*. That's how humans are inherently inertial. We optimize for avoiding change due to fear of the unknown. In some cases, it's wise to stick with what we know works. But in others, this fear prevents us from creating new opportunities and compelling experiences.

As you think about your vision for living an inspired life, be aware that there is likely a significant gap between where you are now and where you want to be—it's true for just about every single person on the planet! If you wake up each morning with a prevailing sense of bliss that continues with you throughout the day until you lay your head on your pillow, congratulations! You don't currently need to change a single thing in your life. But for the rest of us, doing something differently could help us get closer to the vision we established earlier in this book.

It takes courage to drive change. It might not be quite like running into a burning building, but when there's a lot on the line, it can certainly feel like a life-or-death situation. In truth, some decisions absolutely will expose you to a significant amount of risk—emotionally, financially, and otherwise. If things go wrong, it can make your situation worse instead of better. This can be incredibly scary—so scary that you might decide to stick with your inertia and stay on the same course. Although that would mostly likely be easier in the moment, making such a decision from a place of fear will drastically reduce your options and experiences in life. Some of the choices that come with the greatest upsides require a total shake-up of your routine. In other words, you *will not* get what you want most if you continue to do exactly what you are doing today.

Have a voice

Expressing a point of view is often quite scary. It requires a degree of confidence and often conjures up that voice we all have in our head that tells us our perspective isn't "good enough," "well thought through enough," or "important enough" to warrant pushing past the fear of sharing. This is particularly true in settings where we perceive that others in the discussion are, for whatever reason, more qualified to render an opinion (e.g., they're older, more educated, richer, louder; they sound more confident). It's these beliefs that often stop us from speaking up. But if we don't start or weigh in on a discussion, it's nearly impossible to affect the outcome. And if we don't affect outcomes, then nothing ever changes for us.

I saw this dynamic front and center in my consulting days. I can clearly recall meetings early in my McKinsey career where I'd be in a group discussion with very senior client executives. There would often also be a senior McKinsey partner in the meeting, but otherwise, our team would comprise a number of fairly junior consultants. As the conversations unfolded, I remember being blown away that there were peers of mine, in some cases colleagues in their early 20s who were five to 10 years younger than me, weighing in with a point of view or humbly challenging an executive's point of view in ways that helped push the thinking forward. I remember thinking, "Who are these young people to believe they have a better perspective than a 50-year-old Fortune 500 executive?"

But that way of thinking just showed my own imposter syndrome. In these meetings, most of the time, I was convinced that there was no way my perspective could ever be more thoughtful than that of these older, richer, more experienced executives. I figured that my best course of action was to stay quiet and not screw up or say something stupid. That old saying would go through my mind a lot: "Better to be thought a fool than to open one's mouth and remove all doubt." As you can imagine, this story I told myself was fully grounded in the fear of looking bad and in an insecurity of not being as good as everyone else. This put me in a particularly hard spot because it would be very difficult to be a great consultant if I were too afraid to express a point of view. Although I often lacked confidence, I realized that for certain topics, I actually did know more than a CEO ever could because I was immersed in the issue every day, whereas they were a mile wide and an inch deep. I could say things that moved the conversation forward in productive ways, if I only had the courage to act.

Luckily, I realized fairly quickly that most people are actually just "making it up" as they go through life. Some may have a bit more experience on which to base a perspective, or perhaps a deeper education in a particular area, but very often the question or issues that arise around a given topic are new to them. In those situations, most people just make it up as they go along and do the best they can to navigate. They may assert a level of confidence that leads others to believe they have it all figured out, but in so many cases, they really don't. They're just making the best call or expressing the most thoughtful perspective they can based on what they know, but that perspective may or may not be right.

This behavior goes all the way up to the highest levels of leadership, whether in the private sector or government, or parents running a household. When you're in charge, you're often asked to make a call on something with less than perfect information and lacking confidence in your decision. You do the best you can to fill in gaps in your knowledge with input from others, but it's ultimately up to you to decide how to move forward. This should not be confused with knowing the "right" answer—or that a single right answer even exists.

As soon as I realized this and was able to internalize it, it fully changed how I thought about expressing my point of view. I didn't need to be 100 percent sure that I was right or have irrefutable proof of something. Instead, I began to feel more confident speaking up to simply to share my thoughts and start a dialogue. I could pressure test my perspective through conversation, build on it, or even shoot it down. I learned that, either way, sharing ideas always had a way of moving conversations forward constructively.

Even more than that, I felt like people noticed me more whenever I spoke up. By making my voice heard, people got to know me better. I found my relationships strengthening, and more doors began to open for me.

It's funny because I hadn't really experienced this kind of reluctance to share my point of view outside a professional setting, but it dawned on me how the fear of judgment and rejection can cause people to sacrifice their voice in all areas of their life. Instead of taking a stance on what they want, people are influenced by others when it comes to choosing a profession to pursue, what school to attend, what political beliefs to support, and whom they choose as a life partner—or even if they choose a life partner at all.

There is no shortage of individuals out there who will tell you how to live your life. Without the courage to form and express your own point of view, it's very often the case that you find yourself just accepting what someone else is asserting, as that's the easier and less-frightening path to take. It's this outcome that we are fighting to avoid—and where courage plays a critical role in helping you create the inspiring life you deserve to have.

Be authentic

In addition to having the courage to express what we *think*, it also takes enormous bravery to express how we *feel*. So much of our lives revolves around putting on an act to ensure we come across to others in a certain way. The act we put on is of course heavily influenced by those around us, particularly those from whom we seek favor. However, this very often results in us living an inauthentic life in which the image we convey to others is very often not the real version of us that we know exists inside. Every one of us has fears, insecurities, doubts, and oftentimes skeletons in our closet that we don't want others to see. As such, we often find the easier path is to exude a version of ourselves that we think others will like and admire. The older we get, the more cemented this "act" becomes. In fact, it can become hard for us to take a step back and peel apart the real us from the person we put out there for others to see.

The more misaligned these two versions are, the more difficult it will be to craft a life that's inspired and fulfilling, if for no other reason than a large amount of energy that could go into building the life you want ends up going into perpetuating the version of yourself you want others to see.

Showing up in a fully authentic way is infinitely more rewarding, but it requires you to be vulnerable. This is often much scarier for people than putting themselves at risk of physical harm.

"Courage is not just the stone-faced marine," says Dr. Colleen Cira. "It's also sobbing your eyes out and spilling your heart to some-one." Colleen has seen how actions that society often classifies as weaknesses are actually acts of courage. This is especially true when it comes to emotional honesty. "A lot of people don't go there because they don't believe they will recover. They can't let themselves cry," she asserts.[12] It takes true courage to show up authentically regard-less of how people might respond to you. But to live an inspired life, you must be true to yourself.

Insecurities often hold people back from being fully authentic. I took a multi-day course when I was in my early 30s that was focused on helping attendees identify the "stories" they had in their minds that were holding them back and then providing tools and frame-works for getting past those stories. One of the most powerful parts of the course was the realization that each of the 300 people in the room had the same kinds of core insecurities and fears (e.g., not good enough, smart enough, experienced enough). It didn't matter if they were a leading cancer surgeon at the Mayo Clinic or a day laborer struggling just to make it from one day to the next; everyone in the room had some sort of "issue" that was holding them back. Their story played over and over again in their head regardless of whether there was an ounce of truth in it. (And, unsurprisingly, just about everyone felt uncomfortable talking about their story!)

It shocked me to learn that we all share this struggle to feel worthy in some way. And a lot of the insecurities people carry with them have to do with core parts of their experience. For me, I always felt some degree of "less than" when I compared myself with people in my professional network. I was a public-school kid, and then I attended what some in my circle dismissively called a "party school" even though I'd worked my butt off there to get my engineering degree. I wasn't as athletic as others I knew, and I was already beginning to lose some of my hair in my late 20s, so I felt less attractive than others I was around. I had never worked for a "marquee" brand-name company, unlike so many others I knew, and so on.

It was easy for me to identify plenty of things about myself that made me feel like I was falling short, but in this course, I was seeing people who were miles ahead of me in achievement struggling with their version of the same story. And then it hit me: We all have things we're good at and things we're not. We'd all made decisions and followed paths in life that were better than some but perhaps not as "inspiring" as others. We all were worried about whether we'd ultimately be "successful," in whatever dimension that meant (e.g., relationships, wealth, home, career). As soon as I realized this, an enormous weight was lifted from me. I am exactly who I am, and I am clearly not who I am not. There's no point in worrying about what other people think about the real me because it's not up for debate.

Whenever you find yourself facing—or even just imagining—pressure from others to show up a certain way, tap back into the real you. Remind yourself that we are all different, and we do not want the same things. What makes someone else happy will not necessarily make you happy. Don't follow the path you think people want you to take. Follow the path that feels right for the real you. Disappoint 100 people before you're willing to disappoint yourself.

How to reduce your fear

Instead of just focusing on how to manifest more courage, sometimes the path of least resistance is to make situations less scary. Luckily, there are a variety of strategies that will help you become more comfortable with making changes, as well as tactics for lessening your exposure to risk.

Look for opportunities to get into the game early. As an introvert, my first years working as a consultant were especially difficult. I found myself in countless team meetings where it felt like everyone was talking around me. I had ideas that I thought the group would be interested in and would benefit the conversation, but I frequently felt too shy to speak up—especially if there were a lot of people in the room. The longer the meeting went on, the more pressure I felt to say something profound. As the stakes went up, I got even more intimidated and shut down even more.

One day, a key mentor of mine pulled me aside and asked me why I hadn't participated in the meeting we had just finished. He knew I had thoughtful perspectives and that I'd been working on a portion of the topic for a few weeks, so he wanted to know why in the world I hadn't spoken up. My answer went something like, "Well, I was planning to say X, but then Diana said that, so I missed my chance. Then I was going to opine on Y, but the client seemed to believe something different, so I didn't want to contradict them. And then 45 minutes into the meeting, when I hadn't yet contributed, I found myself filtering all my thoughts with a view that 'whatever I say had better be *profound* because it's going to be the first time the group hears my voice.' And of course, that raised the bar too high, and I let the meeting go without saying a word."

My mentor responded with, "Help me understand which of these two scenarios feels more comfortable to you:

"Scenario 1: There are two seconds left on the clock in a basketball game. Your team is two points down. The coach believes in you and wants you to take the ball when it gets inbounded and make the three-pointer for the win just as the buzzer sounds. You haven't actually shot a basket all day, but you have a track record of being a good three-point shooter.

"Scenario 2: The game is about to start. The score is 0-0. The first play has someone on the team throw you the ball as you're running down the court for an easy two-point layup. And no one will likely remember that play."

For me, the answer was easy: give me Scenario 2 every day! Yes, I'd love to be the hero who won the game, but the pain of being the one who lost the game by throwing an airball as the buzzer ran out was just too much stress for me. "Perfect!" my mentor said, "your job is to 'get on the board' with some layups in every meeting you're in."

Once you're in the game, and "on the board," even if you don't make another comment the entire time, you've made a contribution to the success of the game (meeting). And, by the way, when you make that first two-point shot, the adrenaline starts to flow, your confidence begins to build, and you're "one of the team" and not an outside observer, so the next few points will come a lot easier. And perhaps if you do enough of this, having the chance to shoot the winning basket (make a thoughtful contribution well into a meeting) becomes exciting, because even if the contribution doesn't work, you've made so many other ones that you're safe and are important to the game (meeting).

This feedback to me was profound. It was a very simple tip to get in the game when the stakes were lowest, when no one else even had a chance to express a more thoughtful point of view. The first few minutes of a meeting is when even saying something akin to "I noticed the sun comes up in the east" has to be met with some acknowledgement of truth, because people are just getting started.

I immediately made it a point to share something early on in every meeting. I stopped filtering myself with judgment on whether my contribution would blow people away because I knew it didn't have to. As I put this strategy into action, I found that all my mental energy went into advancing the conversation instead of running the never-ending, circular story in my head: "You missed your chance; now you better be brilliant; these other people are so much smarter; what if you say the wrong thing and look like a fool?" That narrative is absolutely worthless, but all of us have a version of it in our heads. Finding ways to overcome these kinds of stories that we tell ourselves can be difficult, but having good timing can help. The sooner you can chime in during a discussion, the less scary it will be to share your thoughts when it really matters.

Determine the true downside. One of my colleagues at McKinsey was a marine, and he was an excellent person to be around whenever things started to get hairy at work. If people were nervous about a presentation, he would remind us that no one was going to die if things didn't go perfectly. Maybe the PowerPoint deck wouldn't be as pretty as it could be, or someone might leave out a slide, but it wouldn't be that big a deal because we would all still go home to our families and our nice, warm beds. This associate had plenty of experience dealing with circumstances in which death was an actual risk if someone made the wrong decision, and he reminded us that we should take comfort in the fact that this was *not* that kind of situation. Talk about perspective!

As you think about risk, it's important to rate the downside honestly and in proportion. In many cases, it's easy to amplify it, which makes things seem scarier than they should be. When you find yourself worrying about the future or having spiraling negative thoughts, it can be helpful to be as objective as possible and determine what the true downside is. Write down all the potential outcomes—the terrible ones, the ideal ones, and everything between. From there, assign percentages for the likelihood of each option happening. You might be surprised by how the odds are overwhelmingly in your favor, which will help you reduce your anxiety around that particular situation. And if the odds aren't looking good after this exercise, you can always decide that the downside isn't worth it. It's a win either way.

Be thoughtful about whom you get advice from. It's helpful to gain insight from others, but a few high-quality perspectives are better than a potpourri of advice you can't make sense of. Go to people you admire who have built a life like the one you want to live, or go to those who are excelling in an area that aligns with your challenge. Other people might give you advice for something you don't care about. Many people will also be prone to giving you advice that is based in fear, since so many people are afraid of change. Though such direction comes from a good place, if you act on it, it will keep you from making choices that will help you live an inspired life.

Have a financial buffer. Some of the toughest choices are tied to money, whether it comes to making it or spending it. Going back to the chapter on financial flexibility, having some savings built up can go a long way toward reducing fear. If you know you can cover your expenses for a few months, you are likely to find yourself making decisions that are not rooted in fear. (If you take a new job and hate it, you aren't stuck. You can put in your two weeks and look for something else.)

Don't burn bridges. There is always the possibility that after embarking on a new path to your true north, you decide you want to return to the old one. This happens all the time in every area of life—and it is by no means a sign of failure. If you realize you were happier or more fulfilled doing what you did before you made a big change, it's great to have the option of reverting to your previous path. This is one reason why it's in your best interest to avoid burning bridges. Whether you're leaving a job, industry, or any other situation, do it thoughtfully and with kindness. Not only is it the right thing to do, but it gives you the peace of mind that you could potentially circle back if you change your mind later.

How to make tough decisions

Courage is often needed the most when you find yourself choosing between very different paths that each have their own major benefits and potential risks. Whenever this happens, a good strategy is to trust your gut. Imagine yourself 10 or 20 years later reflecting back on your current situation. How would you feel if you hadn't taken the initiative to step into an opportunity? If you think you might regret your choice, take that as a sign that you should summon the courage to change your path. But if you don't think you will have any regrets, you might want to stay where you are.

It's important to note that courage does not always mean changing course. When you have the opportunity to step away from what you're doing and try something new, the right answer is not always going to be to take it! Sometimes the better choice is turning down the opportunity. This choice also requires courage. There are trade-offs with every difficult decision, and choosing to stay on the same path is a decision in itself. Don't feel like you haven't acted with courage if you have fully evaluated an alternative path and turned it down because it doesn't align with your vision for living an inspired life.

My goal for this chapter isn't to convince you to try every new thing that comes your way. It's to help you get past any fear that might be holding you back from making the best decision to support an inspired life.

With this in mind, timing is an important thing to consider. Take the time you need to feel comfortable making a decision but know that if you wait until you're 100 percent confident, you will probably never get there. After all, there is rarely full certainty in anything (other than death and taxes). When making any decision that truly matters in your life, you will need to summon some degree of courage.

In general, I've seen that most people wait too long to make a decision. Delaying a decision is a choice in itself because you are choosing to keep doing the same thing rather than doing something different. This comes with an opportunity cost. While you continue with inertia, opportunities can blow right past you. Even if it's not an opportunity that seems to be tied to a specific deadline, do not be fooled. The longer you wait to make a major change, the more difficult it tends to become. This is counterintuitive, since it seems like the more experienced you are, the easier things will be. But this is typically not the case with major changes in your life direction because the older you get and the longer you've been doing things a certain way, the more jarring it becomes to do them differently.

When it comes to professional changes, time is certainly not on your side. The longer you work in a certain industry or role or for a single company, the more opposition you will encounter when changing courses. It's easier to get pigeonholed as a certain type of worker the more time you've spent just doing that one thing. People come to know you as an expert in that field, and it can be harder to transition to something else. Every year you delay making a change will take you one year longer to build a similar level of expertise in another area. And as the years go by, the prospect of change becomes increasingly intimidating.

This is how "later" sometimes never comes. The longer people put things off, the less likely they are to do them. Life gets in the way, and years or even decades pass by in the blink of an eye. Eventually, people realize that making the change they had been considering for many years has become too costly or difficult. Don't let this happen to you.

If you truly believe there are prerequisites to making an important decision, establish a plan and a timeline for completing those actions. Give yourself time to mull it over, do more research, and educate yourself however you see fit. But don't let this process drag on longer than it should. If you find yourself in that situation, there's a good chance you are letting fear dictate your actions.

What to do if you're deadlocked

There will be times when you find yourself at a crucial fork in the road, and even if you implement the strategies in this chapter, along with any others in your toolbox, you still cannot determine which way to go. Both routes will require courage, and you don't want to delay making a decision any longer—but you are unable to decide which path to take.

Many years ago, I was faced with the difficult decision of leaving my 14-year career at McKinsey to take a role at Google. I had worked incredibly hard at McKinsey, built an extensive network, and invested a lot in making partner and being successful in that role—not to mention that I liked my job and they were paying me well. It seemed risky and possibly even stupid to walk away from all that. But at the same time, Google was headhunting me, and the prospect of working there was incredibly compelling. I had every reason to believe I would enjoy that job and find success there just like I had at McKinsey.

I was chatting with a friend about this dilemma, and she shared a perspective with me that I have since utilized many times in my life. She said that a philosophy she subscribes to is "when faced with making a difficult decision, choose the one that makes for a better story." Maybe it's because I'm an adventurer at heart, but I immediately loved this approach. I imagined myself sitting on my couch at home in 25 years reflecting with friends on our careers. I then imagined what it would feel like to be talking about the amazing 25 years I had at McKinsey; then I imagined talking about what an amazing career I'd had with my 14 years at McKinsey and then perhaps another 10 years at Google. As I reflected on what it would feel like to tell each of these stories, I could just feel it inside that the second story would almost certainly be a lot more interesting. It resonated with me so much that it tipped the scales for deciding to accept the job at Google. Since the jobs were otherwise pretty similar in terms of upsides and risks, at least I could count on having a more interesting story by switching things up.

The most inspired lives are often rich with many layers and variety in experiences. Choosing the more interesting story is a way to gain exposure to new things that broaden your horizons. You will form new relationships, develop unexpected skills, and gain exposure to different perspectives. All this can be incredibly valuable in ways you might not see coming. That's why choosing the more interesting story isn't just about having an experience that would be intriguing to others; it's about cultivating a life that sparks your own engagement.

Following your true-north path to live your most inspired life takes a great deal more courage than most people think. That's because you will be making choices that are different than those of the people around you, which will undoubtedly feel uncomfortable at times and terrifying at others. But it's worth it.

Ultimately, courage is a testament to determination, resiliency, and strength. It is an acknowledgment that fear, though a natural and instinctive response, does not define your actions or dictate the course of your life. To live a more inspiring life, you will need to embrace the unknown, transcend limitations, and pursue what truly matters.

Stay focused on your goals and vision, and make sure you are giving them more weight than you are to any fears that crop up along the way. This is how you will not only unlock your full potential but also inspire others to do the same.

CHAPTER 9

Seeing the silver lining

When Rick Werry was in his 20s, he was looking forward to everything life had to offer. He had recently married his high-school sweetheart, and it seemed like the life of his dreams was coming to fruition.

He and his wife wanted a new home of their own, but they didn't have much money. Rick was working in construction at the time, and he heard about a program that guided people through building their own house, a process that made home ownership more affordable. It seemed like the perfect opportunity. Rick and his wife selected a beautiful lot with a big yard in a subdivision outside Salt Lake City. With snowcapped Utah mountains as their backdrop, they began building their dream home.

Everything was going as planned until one day when Rick was using a nail gun to finish a project on the first floor. Instead of shooting the nail smoothly into the wooden beam, it bounced off a knot and shot backwards right into Rick's hand. His friend quickly stepped in to pull the nail out, but Rick saw that he had a gaping hole in the web of skin between his thumb and first finger, and he started to feel queasy. He had never passed out before, but he thought he should grab a drink and sit down for a minute to center himself. He turned to walk across the floor but only made it a few steps before he was struck by a wave of dizziness and passed out. This shouldn't have been a huge problem, but Rick was in exactly the worst possible place when it happened: right next to a hole in the floor that didn't have a staircase built into it yet. He fell through the hole and landed on his neck.

"I can't feel my legs!" he screamed up from the basement floor. He would soon learn he was paralyzed from the chest down.

Going from being a highly active person and having full independence to being wheelchair bound is something most of us can't even imagine. For Rick, it was horrible. He felt like all his dreams had been crushed in an instant. He would never play sports, have kids, be able to work, or take care of himself and his family. If all that was gone, what was left? No matter how hard he tried, he just couldn't picture things getting better. He felt like his life was no longer worth living.

After three months of being in the hospital's ICU and finally going home, Rick was so depressed that he almost took his life. He wheeled himself to a rushing river and sat there thinking about whether he should just roll himself in.

Thankfully, he ultimately decided against it and turned around and went home. He found the courage to take it day by day and see if there would be a silver lining to his experience. He had an outpouring of support from his wife, family, friends, and community. In fact, he was surrounded by people who showed up for him when he needed them the most. And slowly, he regained some mobility and relearned how to do simple things he wasn't able to do right after the accident, such as get himself snacks from the kitchen and type on a keyboard.

Days turned into years, and today Rick is in a totally different place in his life. He and his wife are still happily married, and they have twin boys that keep them very busy. Rick discovered a passion and talent for wheelchair rugby, which helped him get active again, enjoy some friendly competition, and make lifelong friends who can relate to him on a deep level. Rick's team was so good last year that they played in the national championship game! For work, Rick left construction and now works remotely as a natural-resource specialist for the Natural Resource Conservation Service.

Rick understands how far he's come—from both an emotional and a physical standpoint. Thinking back to that day he almost took his life and realizing everything he would have missed ignited a new sense of purpose for him: suicide prevention. These days, you can find Rick sharing his story with auditoriums full of young people and talking about the importance of resiliency. He tells them how important it is to keep going even when things get bad. Rick is so passionate about this topic that he also wrote a book about it, titled *Red Letter Days*. (A nurse at the hospital taught him that every day he was able to accomplish something he couldn't do the day before was a "red letter" day.) Since the accident, Rick has had many red letter days.

Life looks different than what Rick expected, but that's often par for the course. Although he wouldn't have chosen to be in a wheelchair, his life is rich in countless ways. He has meaningful relationships, gratifying hobbies, and work that gives him a sense of purpose, and he has managed to accomplish a number of major items on his bucket list. Despite his seemingly bleak prospects right after the accident, Rick is now living an inspired, fulfilled life.[13]

Every cloud has a silver lining. Sometimes it's hard to see, and it might even take years to find and fully appreciate it, but it's there. Throughout your journey, you will have highs and lows that strike you at your core. You'll cry tears of happiness and sadness—perhaps even at the same time. You'll have moments you will want to exist in forever and others you wouldn't wish on your worst enemy. As a human being, these are all life experiences you can count on having. The hardness of the butter is proportional to the softness of the bread.

This dichotomy is easy to rationalize when you aren't in the moment, but experiencing the low lows in real time can be painful enough to stop you dead in your tracks. You might question all your actions leading up to that point and wonder if there's anything you can do to come out of the situation whole, or even happy. The urge to wallow in how unfair things are might be overwhelming, but the truth is that nothing in life is guaranteed. You can't always control what happens, but you can choose how you react. Good things can come out of every low moment. It's up to you to recognize this opportunity and do what you can to tap into the silver lining.

Beyond that, remember that following your true north and living your most inspired life is not supposed to be about always being happy. Not only is that an unattainable goal, but also many of the things in life that bring us short bursts of happiness do not take the place of more meaningful or fulfilling endeavors. The relationships, activities, and accomplishments that resonate the deepest often take hard work and sacrifice. If you were thinking this journey was always going to be easy, I'm sorry to disappoint you! Even if you're doing everything right, sometimes it will be a struggle. But that just makes your progress more rewarding.

Serendipity

The world is a mysterious place. We can do our best to prepare for success and set ourselves up to have the best possible chance at getting what we want, but there's no escaping the innate element of randomness. If you look at individual events that have impacted your life, you're likely to see that a handful of unexpected occurrences and coincidences played an oversized role in leading you to where you are today. This happens through chance meetings with strangers that turn into best friends, romantic partners, or business partners. It also occurs after stumbling into life-changing opportunities that you were privy to thanks to being in the right place at the right time. Some of these chance encounters stem from missing out on another opportunity. Looking back, you wouldn't have reached the great outcome you have today if everything had gone according to plan. That's the effect of the silver lining.

The first time I experienced this in a major way was when I was 15 years old. I'd borrowed my dad's bicycle and ridden it to a friend's house for the afternoon and left it in the front yard without locking it up. Sure enough, it ended up getting stolen. My dad then did what any parent does when they want to teach their child a lesson about money and responsibility: he said I had to buy him a new bike.

A few days later, I was wandering through town on foot (because I no longer had wheels to borrow!) when I saw a bike that looked a lot like my dad's Schwinn, except it had been stripped of all its most valuable—and easily sellable—parts, including the wheels, handlebars, and brakes. They had been ripped off in such a hurry that what remained of the bike looked a lot like garbage. I stepped a little closer to get a better look. It was definitely my dad's bike. It was in such a sorry state that I almost left it there. But I scooped it up like one would an injured animal and carried it home to see if I could bring it back to good health.

My dad took one look at the mangled mess of metal and sent me to the Schwinn shop in town to figure out how to fix it. I talked to some of the salespeople and started buying the parts I thought I needed. Slowly, I figured out how to make the repairs. On the third week of going to the Schwinn shop to talk about how to fix the bike, the owner of the store happened to be there. He asked me what I was doing since he hadn't yet heard the story but had seen me coming in every few days to buy parts. After I told him what had happened, he said, "You've pretty much built an entire bike at this point; would you like a job building bikes for us?" By that point, I'd realized that I actually loved working on bikes, so I was happy to take the offer.

That job ended up playing an important role in my personal development because it helped me tap into my talent for building and fixing things with my hands. I was able to embrace my fascination of working parts, which ultimately helped me gain the confidence to work on airplane engines and get my degree in engineering. It also helped me earn money in a job that was way more interesting than the fast-food jobs some of my friends had, which served to help pay for my early flying lessons at the local airport.

If my dad's bike hadn't gotten stolen, I wouldn't have identified my passion and developed my skills as quickly. That means I wouldn't have been presented with the same opportunities or had the preparation to capitalize on them and wouldn't have had the money I needed to fund some of my earliest flying experiences. The butterfly effect could have made me end up in a totally different place from where I am today. It ended up being serendipitous that the theft of my dad's bike would lead me to the exact place I needed to be.

When things don't go as planned, it helps to think about serendipity. You might not get what you want in the moment, but something even better might be right around the corner. Regardless of whether you believe in fate, karma, or anything else about destiny, open yourself up to the opportunities and experiences that come from being on an unexpected path. It's much easier to do so when you have a positive attitude. When you find yourself on an unexpected path, lean into workshopping alternative options and solutions instead of complaining or lamenting your lot in life.

Your relationship with failure

On your path to living your most inspired life, you should aim high. In doing so, you might not always reach your goal—and that's not just OK; it's to be expected.

We all fail, but the way we view failure makes a huge difference in how we move forward. Seeing failure in a positive light can be challenging, but it's also a mindset that can lead to personal growth, resilience, and future success. Here's where making the effort to become a "glass-half-full" type of person really pays off. The sooner we can spring back into action after a setback, the quicker we will experience the payoffs.

Here are some simple strategies to help you have a more productive relationship with failure:

> **Check in with yourself.** Do you feel like you failed because you disappointed yourself, or someone else? Other people's definitions of success are likely different from your own. Make sure you're focusing on your own unique goals and vision, rather than letting other people cloud the way you feel about your choices, progress, and accomplishments.

> **Change your perspective.** Instead of viewing failure as a dead end, see it as a stepping stone to success. Every failure is an opportunity to learn and improve, which gets you closer to your goal. Embrace it as a valuable experience that can teach you important lessons. As my friend Loree Draude says, "'FAIL' stands for 'first attempt in learning.'"

> **Focus on learning.** Shift your focus from the outcome to the process. Ask yourself what you've learned from the failure, how it can inform your future decisions, and what skills you've gained. Such a mindset encourages continuous self-improvement.

> **Embrace resiliency.** The more you fail, the stronger you get. Leveraging failure as a chance to build your resiliency can help you face challenges with greater confidence and adaptability.

➤ **Celebrate effort.** Acknowledge the effort you put into your endeavors, regardless of the outcome. Celebrating your commitment and hard work can help you maintain a positive attitude and see progress for what it is.

➤ **Prioritize logic over emotion.** Treat failure as a form of feedback on your approach, not a reflection of your worth. Don't beat yourself up. (Doing so is rarely productive!) Instead, analyze what went wrong, what you could have done differently, and how you might adjust your strategy next time.

Failure is a natural part of life. We all fail every single day. Sometimes it's small things such as making a wrong turn or forgetting to send an email. Other times it's bigger things, such as not taking care of our health or failing to maintain relationships that matter to you. Failure can be the hardest to deal with mentally when an action ends up having an oversized impact that lasts for years, or even decades. In those situations, finding the silver lining is necessary for getting back on the right path in life.

When Jason Spyres was a teenager, he was sentenced to 30 years in prison for the non-violent crime of selling cannabis. He ended up serving 15 years.

While he was locked up, he felt all the emotions you would expect a young person to feel in that situation: despair, regret, panic, humiliation. But he also felt hopeful. He was watching the prison TV one day when he saw an interview with a Stanford University admissions officer who spoke about how impressed she was with candidates who were able to accomplish so much with very few resources. It made him wonder if maybe he could get into Stanford someday.

"I looked around my room and asked, 'What resources do I have?'" Jason recalled. "I have a pencil and an 8½x11 writing pad. I have stamps and a prison library card."[14]

He decided to put those resources to work and learn as much as possible while incarcerated. He checked out books on economics, chemistry, physics, and calculus. He didn't have a calculator, so he taught himself to do advanced math without one. He would have loved to take educational classes offered through the prison, but due to Illinois prison policies at the time, his offense declared him legally "unrehabilitatable" and indirectly unable to participate when he arrived at prison. Jason did the most with what he had. His mom turned him on to a program she'd heard about called Khan Academy, a free online educational platform that helped fill in the gaps in the prison's library.

Jason knew that Stanford was a long shot for most students, so he did everything possible to set up himself up for success. He studied six hours a day just about every day. His efforts paid off. In 2017, Jason was finally released. He used Khan Academy's SAT prep and was accepted into Stanford University.

Jason's experience with the criminal-justice system helped him realize how important access to education is for all people, regardless of their ability to pay for school or attend in person. Jason is now the CEO of TAP (Training All People), where he uses technology to give vocational skills to others. He believes that all people are teachable and that all people, whether they are in a prison cell or an Ivy League school, deserve to share in the benefits that technology brings to education.[15]

When Jason was locked up, he'd lost his freedom, but no one could take away his hope that something good could come out of his situation. He refused to let one failure define him—no matter how big that failure seemed. He embodies what it means to find the silver lining.

Jason Spyres with Sal Khan, the founder of Khan Academy, which provided
Jason with a pathway from prison to Stanford.

Though my life story doesn't have anything nearly as challenging
as Jason's in it, as I've looked back over the many years of my journey, I'm amazed at how many things have happened that at the
time were major sources of disappointment or frustration but in
hindsight were some of the best things to ever happen to me. Having a color-vision deficiency kept me out of the airlines, but that
opened up so many other flying adventures and different career
paths that never would have happened had I been hired by a major

airline as I'd dreamed about so many years ago. Had I gotten the job at Arco that I applied for in business school because they had operations in Alaska, I never would have taken a consulting job in Boston that eventually led me to McKinsey. Had I gotten the promotion at one of my earlier jobs that I'd really wanted, the cost of leaving that job to take another one likely would have been too high and I likely would have succumbed to the fear of "taking a step backward" economically. Fortunately, I didn't get that promotion, which opened the door for a much more exciting career journey. In the end, I've counted more than a dozen "significantly disappointing moments" in my life that resulted in great, unexpected things coming my way. At this point, I've been able to see any disappointment that emerges as simply the signal that something else even cooler is in my near future. It's a story I tell myself that is true more often than not, and even if it turns out not to be, seeing the silver lining in something disappointing just helps me feel better and puts me in a frame of mind to make the most of every situation I find myself in.

As you continue on your true-north path, look for the silver lining in every situation. It can be minor low points, such as not landing the client you wanted, not getting the raise or promotion you're sure you deserve, having to go on that business trip you try to avoid every year, or major events such as losing a loved one or being diagnosed with a terminal illness. Instead of focusing on the negatives, train yourself to look for the positives. This very often takes intentional effort and doesn't mean you shouldn't take the time to feel sad or grieve a loss. But after taking the time to process your disappointment, you'll want to start looking for opportunities that stem from the situation you find yourself in. Ask yourself how you can make the most of it. Sure, there might only be a 5-percent upside, but enjoy it nevertheless! The more often you do this, the more naturally it will come. Over time, you will become less bothered by minor setbacks and inconveniences and less stressed about situations you can't control. You'll start to realize that you have enormous power to turn negatives into positives and will harness this power to create amazing things in not only your life but also the lives of those around you.

CHAPTER 10

Assessing and recalibrating

No path to an inspired life stays the same forever. Even when we are intentional and thoughtful about our choices, circumstances change. We evolve. What we want is inherently a moving target over time. That's why it's so important to be thoughtful and deliberate around navigating changes.

There are two key failure modes around change, and I see people operating in these modes all the time:

> **Changing paths too quickly and frequently.** People go down a path that ends up being harder than they'd anticipated. They get frustrated, hit some roadblocks, and decide to quit. They give up early because they are overwhelmed or burned out or stop believing that this route could end up providing the inspiration and fulfillment they desire. As a result, they don't reach their goal, and they end up floating around picking new goals and moving on from them before they reach them, thereby continuing the same vicious cycle.

> **Not changing paths enough.** People get stuck in inertia and go on too long (sometimes forever) doing the same thing, whether

they still feel inspired by it or not. They get into steady-Eddie mode and just maintain the status quo, which is somewhat comfortable but usually also marked by boredom or a feeling of having settled. This mode is often rooted in the fear of the unknown, or a heightened aversion to risk.

Neither of these opposite ends of the spectrum is healthy or productive when it comes to living an inspired and fulfilling life. How do you find a happy medium? Here are five things to consider when thinking about the prospect of change:

1. Seasons

Our lives are ruled by seasons. We're accustomed to going (or sending our kids) back to school in the early fall; we get together with family in winter to celebrate holidays; we take time off in the summer to have fun and relax. In many regions, the weather helps give us clues about what's coming and puts us in the right mood for whatever season is next.

What we often don't realize is that life also comes with "seasons" that are tied to things we're doing in our lives. Raising toddlers is a season (albeit one that's several years long). If you're an accountant, then tax season is something that comes along at the same time every year and typically lasts for several months that lead into the most demanding week of the year. In college, there's finals season when a couple weeks are particularly challenging in terms of the hours spent prepping to convey all you've learned over the course of a semester. Some seasons might be quite a bit longer than these, such as caring for aging parents or earning a PhD. And, like the true seasons we experience over the course of every year, they each have a beginning and an end.

This concept of seasons is a powerful one when you find yourself experiencing periods of frustration or feeling overwhelmed. All too often, people will give up on pursuing a goal, or will walk away from a great opportunity or job, because at that moment there's something about it that feels particularly hard or unsustainable, leading that voice in their head to say, "I can't do this anymore." However, if one were to look at these challenging periods as seasons, one might recognize that, just like winter, each will eventually end and give way to a set of experiences that are more inspiring.

I would see this in consulting all the time when I'd find myself on a project that was requiring 80–100 hours per week of my time. It was very easy to get into the mindset of "I can't take this anymore," which would certainly be true if that reality were going to continue on indefinitely. However, it was virtually always the case that the intensity of the project was at most just a few weeks, or perhaps a couple months, long and then the pace would lighten up dramatically.

By maintaining this perspective on difficulties that you encounter, you can frequently put the challenge in context and find the internal motivation to "get through to spring," much like how seeing the finish line at the end of a long race provides the boost of energy required to make it through.

This concept is a powerful one to internalize because you are sure to encounter challenging periods throughout your entire life. For example, when you're in college, your primary goal is to get good grades and graduate, and everything else has to take a backseat. Since you don't yet have the experience to get a good job or the time to work many hours—if you are working a side job at all—you will probably be poor during that time. That's just the season you're in. Similarly, when you have a young child, your primary goal is likely to be spending time with them and making sure you're there for as many milestones as possible. You might not be able to work fewer hours, so you feel the time crunch in your me time and don't get as much sleep as you would ideally like. Those are just the characteristics of that season.

Sometimes the least desirable aspects of a season can drive you crazy. You will go through particularly down moments when you feel like the struggle is harder than you'd anticipated. You're not really sure it's worth it or whether you even still want what you set out to achieve. These are all fair considerations, but you should also realize that there are natural low points in time for what you're trying to achieve. Although seasons can last for years and feel unending when you're in the thick of one, they do not go on forever. Sometimes you cannot help but sacrifice some areas of your life to fully embrace a season and make the most of it. The key point here is recognizing that these situations are in fact seasons and not a new normal you are expected to uphold for the rest of your life. This is important to keep in mind as you assess your progress, because there's a big difference between a short-term sacrifice and lifetime compromise.

As the parent of a toddler, you might be struggling with that season in general, rather than other aspects of your life that feel particularly difficult during this time. If you can compartmentalize the season, it will help you determine whether you're going through a naturally difficult part of your journey that will end relatively soon (e.g., potty training) or you've veered onto an undesirable path that will keep going unless you do something about it (e.g., you're doing 90 percent of the parenting while your partner sits around watching TV). If your discontentment is par for the course for the season, your best option might be to just tough it out. But if you can rule out the season as the cause of the problem, it's a sign that you have veered away from your true north. Assess things more carefully and consider recalibrating.

2. Trade-offs

Virtually everything in life that we do comes with a series of trade-offs. It's almost never the case that you can have it all: nice weather, great school district, inexpensive housing, low cost of living, short commute, family nearby, and lots of free time and extra money to pursue the hobbies you enjoy. We all compromise every day to get the best balance of the things that matter most to us. Recognizing and accepting this concept of "trade-offs" is very powerful when you're feeling pressure to make changes or feeling less than satisfied with your situation. The key, though, is to ensure that the trade-offs you're making are, in fact, aligned with the life you want to live and the experiences you want to have that leave you inspired and fulfilled.

For example, maybe you've chosen to live in Chicago because your family is there and you have a local job you love. You might hate cold winters, but you prioritize your family and job above living in a milder climate. On those 5° days when the wind is whipping off the lake, complaining about the weather isn't going to magically bring on a heat wave—or make you feel any better. You need to simply acknowledge that you're choosing to prioritize some aspects of your life over others and that this trade-off is worth it. Instead of complaining about winter in Chicago, you could choose to find ways to embrace it: ice skating at the rink, sitting by a warm fire with your family and getting cozy, taking a short vacation to Florida to warm up, etc. In this example, you chose to live in Chicago, so complaining about cold winters is a complete waste of time and would be like waking up every day complaining that the sun rises in the east.

The point here is that you get to choose how you react to the situations you're in, and when you've made certain, intentional trade-offs in your life, it makes no sense to waste time complaining about them if you are still on track and heading toward your true north. When I chose to move to Bend, by definition, I was also choosing to spend more time on the road since my job was located elsewhere. As such, I don't complain at all when I have to travel out of town, even though there are certainly times when I wish I could travel a bit less.

Similarly, when you choose to be a doctor, you are also choosing to be on call several nights each month. When you choose to be a professional actor, you are choosing to get turned down at many auditions, and if you're a highly successful actor, you're choosing to give up a lot of your private life. These things just go together, and you need to recognize this and not waste time complaining about it. If you feel that these trade-offs are no longer acceptable, then do something about it, make a change, and then accept the new trade-offs you've created. The beautiful thing about this is that you are in control and get to decide what you're willing to trade off in order to lead the life you want.

3. Running to, not running from

Over the course of my multi-decade career, I've had many individuals ask for career advice. Very often this happens when the individual has come across a new job opportunity that's forcing them to make a decision, or they're wallowing in a particularly difficult time in their career and are looking for inspiration and guidance on how best to navigate the situation.

A powerful concept that was taught to me early in my career was around the distinction of running to something versus running from something—the idea of course being that it's far more exciting and inspiring to do the former since that connotes a sense of excitement, anticipation, and comfort, whereas running "from" something conveys a sense of fear, or pain, or a need to escape. If we want to live an inspired and fulfilling life, wouldn't we all want to find ourselves running to things that light us up and create the type of inspiration we all want in our lives?

Unfortunately, all too often when speaking with people about making a change, it becomes pretty clear they're running "from" something. Maybe it's the unsustainable hours or a disrespectful boss or a poor corporate culture. Or maybe it's a dysfunctional relationship with a long-time partner. They're at their wits' end and just want out, so they choose to make a change. But guess what often happens. When I check in with them several months later, they might be in a different place or with a different company or in a different relationship, but as I probe into how their life is going, it's mostly not any different than it was before they made the change. This is because it's very often the case that the situation they're running from is one that they created or contributed to themselves, and when they get to their next situation, they realize that the situation ends up being just a different version of the same thing they had before. They were the one common denominator in both situations, and they brought the dysfunction with them, whether that was cultivating poor relationships with colleagues, working long hours, or taking other actions that didn't align with their true north.

They got caught up in the "grass is greener" mentality and just wanted to get away from their current situation rather than invest the time to truly assess whether the change they were taking on was bringing with it the level of inspiration and excitement they were currently missing. This is what running "to" something should bring. And when you run to something, you arrive there with a mindset and enthusiasm that automatically sets you up for a far greater chance of success than simply running away from your current situation would.

4. Stagnation and fear

The first three points are particularly powerful tools for confronting a situation where you're contemplating the need to make a change. As I outlined at the beginning of this chapter, in making these types of decisions, there's a failure mode that can cause individuals to drive too much change, often at the expense of achieving the things they really want in life, and as a result, they fail to build any meaningful level of mastery of something and then burn bridges by bailing out of it before they've contributed anything meaningful. This creates a reputation that is often hard to undo, and over time, it raises the difficulty of creating all the elements required for living an inspired and fulfilling life.

Conversely, the other failure mode is in individuals who are too afraid to make any change and find themselves on the same course throughout their entire life, despite not feeling particularly inspired, fulfilled, or even happy. When nothing is changing in your life as time continues to pass, it's usually not a good thing. It's certainly possible that you originally set off on exactly the right course and truly do want to keep chugging along in exactly the same way toward your goal, but oftentimes people keep doing the same things because they are afraid of trying something else, or afraid of failing, or of looking bad, or any of the myriad natural fears that all of us have.

We all need to watch out for this situation and regularly challenge ourselves to recalibrate regardless of whether we're in fact on the path to our best life and making choices that will give us the experiences and sense of fulfillment we all aspire to have over the course of our lives. If an honest assessment of our situation suggests that perhaps we're stagnant and just going through the motions, then it's absolutely time for a change. Every day that goes by with you sleepwalking through it is a day that could have been spent learning a new skill, meeting a person who inspires you, or taking on a new experience that opens up entirely new frontiers for your life.

5. Choose the better story

In chapter 8, we talked about tips on how to have the courage to make difficult choices. You can use these same techniques when trying to determine whether a change in your life's course or key goals makes sense. When all factors seem equal, or the highs and lows between two opportunities balance each other out, make the choice that will lead to the better story. Variety and adventure add a richness to life that cannot be ignored. If something sounds interesting and would open you up to new experiences you can imagine talking about at a dinner party someday, you might want to give that decision a little more weight. This might sound like an unusual way to make decisions, but I've leveraged this strategy for years, and it's one of my favorite ways to assess opportunities.

No matter who you are or what you have going on right now for your professional and personal life, you have the power to make changes. No one is holding you hostage and making you live a certain way. You could move to a new country, start a new career, or go back to school. You could buy a house or sell your house and live out of a camper or a sailboat. You could adopt a child or a dog—or a child who has a dog. You could end toxic relationships that no longer serve you (regardless of how long you've been in them) and embark on healthier, more rewarding ones. No matter how old you are or how established you are in any particular avenue of life, you will always have the power to establish a new true north and completely reinvent yourself.

You might be thinking, "Sure, someone else might have that kind of freedom, but I don't." I beg to differ. It might be hard to make major life transitions, and there's an element of risk in doing so, but it's entirely possible. You are the master of your own life. With that in mind, you are the person who is responsible for checking in with yourself regularly to make sure you're still on the path you want to be on. Make sure you aren't getting stuck in a state of inertia because you haven't mustered the courage to go after what you really want.

Timing

How often should you assess your life? Sometimes it's hard not to automatically go there after a particularly lousy day, but that is not the right headspace for doing the kind of big-picture, holistic review that will help inform your best next steps.

One of my mentors, Endre Holen, assesses his life and path forward every year on October 29th. Why October 29th, you ask? Because that was the date he had been hired into his job at McKinsey more than 20 years earlier. It might seem odd or quirky to set this particular date, but the reasoning behind it is important. As Endre explained to me, much like all of us in consulting, he had found himself at multiple points during a given year feeling really down about his situation. Perhaps he was working too many hours, or was working with individuals he didn't particularly like, or was working on projects that just weren't very interesting. In those moments, it was very easy to make the decision to quit and do something else. In fact, many of his colleagues did just that. In the "heat of the moment," they let frustration get the best of them and they walked away. In most cases, they were running "from" their current situation.

However, Endre also noticed that during the course of any given year, there were amazing highs. He was working with incredibly talented and motivated individuals; he was getting more thoughtful feedback on improving his skills than he'd ever had; he was traveling to interesting countries all over the world; and he was working on some of the most interesting and impactful challenges with the top companies in the world. In those moments, he couldn't believe he was getting paid to have such amazing experiences.

It was this realization that every year was filled with such highs and lows that led Endre to simply decide not to overreact to either the highs or the lows but instead to take a thoughtful period of introspection each year to calibrate whether it made sense to stay the course. In doing so, Endre would reflect on the prior 12 months and assess whether he felt that, overall, the year had been a good one. Had he grown personally and professionally? Had the positive experiences meaningfully outweighed the negative ones? He'd also look forward and ask himself whether the year ahead was likely to provide a similarly positive outcome. Was he excited about the clients he was likely to work with, or about a pending promotion, or about some research he was going to be leading? If this assessment of both the year in review as well as the year ahead was overall quite positive, then Endre would commit to the next year and put aside any useless and unproductive second guessing of whether he should keep doing what he was doing. He would wait until the next October 29th to do that.

Of course, taking this disciplined approach helps us avoid overreacting in moments of challenge or disappointment and helps us see the totality of our experiences in context. This is not to say that if an opportunity comes along during the year that you shouldn't assess it at that time. Of course you should, but then you'd be looking at that opportunity through the lens of excitement and intrigue and perhaps it would be something you'd run to rather than making a reactive decision to leave during a particularly bad moment in time.

I started doing annual life assessments, and immediately, it was a huge win for me. I stopped getting sucked into daily frustrations and was able to better stay focused on the big picture while remaining open to unexpected opportunities—such as when Google called, and years later when Cisco reached out and enticed me to walk away from a really good situation to pursue something even better.

Lastly, even if it feels like everything is going swimmingly, you should still set aside the time to do your annual review. Of course, it's entirely possible that you are on the right path and don't need to make any adjustments to continue making progress toward reaching your goals. But you won't know that for sure without allowing the time, space, and honesty to check in with yourself.

Endre Holen and Darren Pleasance teaming up to pick up Endre's new plane; Endre never stopped assessing his life and crafting an ever-changing and inspiring life journey.

What should you assess?

A better question might be *what shouldn't you assess*? That's because your life is full of possibility. Start by going back and considering what an inspired life means to you. In chapter 1, you were provided with the following list of elements to consider when shaping your vision:

> ➤ Pursuing passions

> ➤ Mastery

> ➤ Meaningful connections/relationships

> ➤ Being around other people

> ➤ Purpose

> ➤ Home

➤ Physical belongings

➤ Amount of free time

➤ Autonomy

➤ Location

➤ Hobbies/activities that bring you joy

➤ Personal growth

➤ Spirituality

➤ Exercise

➤ Travel

➤ Adventure

➤ Stability

➤ Community

You were asked which of these elements play a crucial role in giving you energy, enthusiasm, and a zest for life. You were asked to identify the ones that need to be part of your daily or weekly routine or incorporated a few times a year. Lastly, you were asked to establish goals around these priorities to help bridge the gap between your current life and your ideal life. Look back at your answers and see if the vision you last established still tracks for you. This will help you determine whether you should continue going after the same goals or establish new ones.

In chapter 2, you created a road map for reaching your goals. Refer back to this and think about the past year. Considering all the hard work you've put in and everything you've learned, are you excited to continue this journey over the course of the next year? Are you building the skills you need to reach your desired end point? Are the hardship and pain worth it?

Also check the time-management tools in chapter 6 and determine how your ideal schedule compares with your actual schedule.

Are there differences that need to be corrected, or do your ideal and reality look fairly similar?

If everything is still lining up, that's great! Recommit to the process and go all in. If, after reaching your goals from the previous year, you have new goals, you'll need to create new road maps to help guide you over the coming year. If you need to make adjustments to your weekly schedule or commitments to get you closer to alignment with where you want to be, figure out how to do that.

Alternatively, if you do this assessment and find yourself at a point where you feel the calling to go in a different direction, that's OK too! It's possible that you've been following your vision for an inspired life yet somehow things just don't feel quite right. You thought you wanted a certain outcome, but now that you've gotten more life experience, you might want something else. That's totally normal. The path to living an inspired life is often a winding one. You set a vision that guides you, but as you learn, grow, and have new experiences, what drives your inspiration is likely to evolve. You don't have to get it all right when you are in your 20s. It's more about building the muscle to have awareness in what you're doing and continually assessing whether your choices are still right for you. Don't think about it as failure or taking a step backward. It's far worse to stay in a situation that no longer feels right to you than to avoid making a change.

Oftentimes, as we gain more experience, we are able to make better choices for our future. Coming up with new ideas, plans, and passions is something that should be celebrated rather than shied away from.

Above all, remember that your life is yours and you are always in the driver's seat. Do not fall asleep at the wheel doing what you've been doing simply because you've failed to recognize that you have other options. To keep heading toward your true north and live a life that is truly inspiring, you need to remain self-aware.

CHAPTER 11

It's the journey

A t this point, you've probably gotten a good sense for my love of aviation! Flying planes has been my passion since childhood.

If aviation isn't your thing, you probably see a plane in the sky and think, "Cool, it has wings; it's in the air; it's going fast; it's not a bird; it's a plane." Pilots see a plane in the sky and notice so much more. The shape of the body, how fast it's traveling, whether it's a single-engine or multi-engine plane, whether it's a piston engine or turbine engine—and from the specific sound of the engine, they can often tell whether it's a vintage plane from years gone by or something more modern. Some planes are light and agile and feel like sports cars in the air. Others are larger, faster, and more powerful, and you can get the exhilaration of seeing the world pass under you at 10 miles per minute. Having flown more than 50 different kinds of airplanes, I can tell you that not all planes are created equal. They're all fun, but some are much cooler than others.

There is one specific kind of airplane that has always stood out to me above the rest: the P-51 Mustang. I first heard that Rolls-Royce Merlin 12-cylinder engine roar past me 40 years ago at an airshow in Reno, Nevada, and it's stuck with me ever since. The P-51 is a thing of beauty. It's an American long-range, single-seat fighter and fighter-bomber that's known for its role in World War II where it helped Allied forces gain air superiority. It's fast and easy to maneuver and was able to outperform the fighter planes of both the German Luftwaffe and the Japanese Navy. The P-51 was used in many conflicts all over the world, and it remained a favorite of many pilots, even when they stopped making them after newer fighter jets were developed. Many of these Mustangs were sold at a surplus after the war, often for as little as $1,500. Today, they are worth over $2 million each—even if the plane is only partially restored. That's in large part because there are fewer than 200 privately owned P-51 Mustangs left in the world.[16]

I had always dreamed of what it would be like to fly the P-51 Mustang. I had seen photos of the cockpit, and I imagined myself sitting in the pilot's seat, my hand on the throttle. I could practically feel what it would be like accelerate down the runway hearing the iconic sound of the 1,500-horsepower Rolls Royce Merlin engine and then race across the countryside at speeds approaching 500 MPH. But I didn't know if I would ever get to experience that in real life. Being able to fly a P-51 is rare—even if you're a highly skilled pilot who has decades of experience. To even qualify to take a Mustang into the air, you have to log a ton of hours flying "tailwheel" aircraft (planes with a small wheel on the back, rather than a "nose" gear), and you have to get time in a similar plane, such as the North American T-6, which would help to provide the experience needed to fly a Mustang safely. I knew getting regular access to a T-6 would not be easy. And even if I figured that out, I would still need to gain access to a Mustang.

Most Mustang owners don't let random pilots take their ultra-valuable baby for a spin around the skies. It's possible to buy your way into the cockpit by going through a company in Florida that charges about $50,000 for a week of lessons in a similar plane. This wasn't appealing to me, not just because of the cost but because I wanted to be able to fly without an instructor on board. Instead of being a forever student, I envisioned flying by myself or taking a friend up to share the experience. Needless to say, the dream of flying a Mustang was very real, but the path to how it might actually happen was quite murky.

I had all this in the back of my mind from the time I was a teenager. I loved flying, and I knew it was a core part of living my most inspired life, whether I did it professionally or as a hobby. Since flying a P-51 was the ultimate fantasy for many pilots, including me, I thought about the steps I would need to take over the course of my life to get there. At times, it seemed like a pipe dream, but nevertheless, I was intentional about my actions, making sure they were consistent and aligned with my goal. I formed relationships that helped me learn and grow, and I kept honing my flying skills over time. During my multi-decade career journey, I remained firmly entrenched in aviation. Slowly, doors began opening for me that could bring me closer to the P-51.

I got into competition aerobatics in my 20s and ended up leading the Northern California Aerobatic Club, growing it to one of the largest chapters in the country. That led to an opportunity to join the Board of the International Aerobatic Club, a division of the Experimental Aircraft Association (EAA). From there, I was asked to join the EAA board, which I still sit on today.

During this time, I was also introduced to the Commemorative Air Force (CAF) and a somewhat abandoned T-6 in Livermore, California, that was looking for a pilot sponsor. It was covered in dust and looked like it had been inactive for some time. I paid the nominal sponsor fee, and the local CAF wing leaned in to get the airplane back up and flying. I was the only pilot for that airplane, so I had an amazing opportunity to amass a bunch of T-6 time over several years until the CAF decided to move the airplane from California to Wisconsin to another CAF wing.

Shortly thereafter, another T-6 owner let several of us with T-6 time simply rent his airplane on an hourly basis. That kept me going with some regular T-6 adventures. Though I had no obvious path to flying a P-51, it was not lost on me that one of the most important prerequisites for flying a Mustang was having a lot of T-6 time. So in addition to being fun, flying the T-6 would help me in the unlikely event that the opportunity to fly a Mustang might someday appear. As a mentor had told me years before, if you want a certain outcome, you need to do things that are consistent with that outcome and be patient. For me, this meant getting as much T-6 time as I could—and being patient.

That patience paid off in 2018 when, at the age of 53, I got a call from a friend of a friend who told me about a museum in Hollister, California, that had a T-6 and P-51 available for members to fly. It was a small organization that had been around since the early 1970s, and they intentionally kept the group small to ensure that the airplanes flew enough but not too much and that they had a good mix of people to create a fun and safe atmosphere, with everyone pitching in to not only fly the airplanes but also clean, maintain, and improve them. A spot had opened up, and I was invited to interview based on the endorsement I had gotten from the same friend who'd helped me get into the CAF T-6 several years earlier. Apparently, the group felt good enough about me to let me into the organization.

Joining the organization was the first step in a multiyear journey toward flying a P-51. Before anyone can fly the Mustang, the group required them to have 100 hours flying any T-6 and 25 hours in the club's T-6. Luckily, I had already made good headway on these hours! From there, I would need to get trained specifically on flying the Mustang, obtain approval from the insurance agency, and pass a flight test to get approval from the FAA. I'll spare you all the details, but this process was not easy, and I made it! After what had been years of intentional work leading up to this exact moment, I was able to take my first solo trip in a P-51 Mustang.

It was everything I'd imagined it would be: the incredible power of the Merlin engine, the sight of the huge propeller disk that covers the sky, and the acceleration straight to 160 knots in the climb. The bubble canopy provides amazing visibility, and the smell and sound of the engine are truly distinctive. As I looked down from my first solo flight, it struck me that this is what thousands of young pilots in WWII would have felt like on their first Mustang flight so many decades earlier. It was all truly incredible.

Though reaching the destination felt great, the journey was even more meaningful. All the learning and growing was a huge part of the process. I got a deep sense of fulfillment from reaching my ultimate goal, but I also got similar levels of fulfillment as I accomplished each milestone along that journey. That's because I knew that during each of those milestones, the ultimate goal of flying a P-51 may, or may not, ever happen. Despite this uncertainty, throughout this journey, I was always "being a P-51 pilot" and taking actions consistent with someday having the opportunity to fly this iconic aircraft. Fortunately, preparation and opportunity converged, and I found myself among the lucky handful of people in the world who get to fly this historic plane.

When we're always thinking about our next move, it's easy to lose sight of how much the journey matters. But that is the day-to-day reality of life. It's getting up in the morning and balancing work, family, friends, hobbies, and exercise and still trying to get enough sleep. That is the dance that goes on for years, so we need to make the most of it. Don't wait to feel inspired and fulfilled. Seek it out every day.

Darren in front of the P-51, the culmination of an over 30-year journey.

Here are some key things to remember when it comes to living an inspired life.

You won't always be happy. It's not about being happy; it's about being fulfilled. This is the experience of feeling proud and content in the life you've led knowing that you've lived your best life and helped others along the way. You should have a disproportionately higher amount of satisfaction than dissatisfaction over time, but there will be ups and downs—and that's what gives texture to your life and deepens your appreciation for the high points.

Inspiration does not need to come from big, grandiose things. Milestone moments and Instagram-worthy occasions get the spotlight when it comes to living an inspired life, but it's often the simple, more private moments that provide the most fuel. Maybe it's waking up in the morning and having a quiet moment to yourself. When you go outside with your cup of coffee to listen to the birds chirp, it centers you and starts your day off right. It doesn't take heroics to make moments like these happen. It just takes a bit of self-awareness and gratitude to help you appreciate and get energy from these less-momentous experiences.

You do not have to be wealthy. Money gives you flexibility to make certain choices, but it certainly does not buy happiness. As we established in earlier chapters, having a lot of money is not correlated with feeling inspired and fulfilled—and in many cases, having too much money leads to a level of stress and complexity that actually diminishes your quality of life. It's not that you can't be wealthy and inspired, because you certainly can. It's also true that you can be someone of very limited financial means but be extremely rich in the experiences and achievements you create in your life.

What you see online isn't real. If you calibrate against the lives you see on the internet, you are setting yourself up to always feel inadequate. It's easy to create an image of happiness and fulfillment on social media. From your friends' posts, you might think they are light-years ahead of you when it comes to crafting an inspired life. But you can't believe everything you see on the internet. Behind every smiling vacation photo are stories of missed connecting flights, crying kids, spats with partners, and food that wasn't very good. No one's life is as perfect as they make it look online, and you shouldn't be comparing your life to others anyway. Your benchmark is you and how you're doing against the goals you've set for the life you want to lead.

People won't always support you, and that's OK. You can make choices that enable you to craft a life that leaves you feeling inspired and fulfilled, but your parents might still think that you should have become a doctor. That's just the reality of living the life that's best for *you*, rather than making choices that are rooted in seeking the approval of others. Hopefully the people who matter most in your life will appreciate and respect your decisions, but you have to accept that they might not. People can get uncomfortable when others make choices that are in opposition to what they have chosen for themselves. They might even think they are doing you a favor by continually trying to talk you into doing something else. This is where your courage comes in. It's OK to be different. If you're feeling satisfied with your life, that's all that matters. Build your chosen "family" by cultivating relationships with people who fully accept you. Also take comfort in the fact that this is a common thing that happens to the most amazing people and that it doesn't mean that you should have compromised your true self to fit in.

You won't ever "arrive." It's easy to think that if you work hard enough, someday you will wake up and think, "This is it! I've made it!" The journey to living an inspired life does not have an end point. You just need to keep seeking out those sources of inspiration that drive you forward and give you the life experiences and outcomes that you want for yourself and those around you. Of course, you'll achieve many milestones in life that are reasons for celebration and that provide a feeling of achievement and fulfillment. But it's the ongoing pursuit of these achievements over a lifetime that ultimately weaves the fabric of a life well lived.

Summing it all up

I talk about a number of concepts in this book, and each of them contributes meaningfully when it comes to heading toward your true north and living your best life. But in the end, the formula for living an inspired and fulfilling life is disproportionally driven by three of these concepts in particular, so it's worth keeping these points front and center as you navigate the journey before you:

> **Spend as much of your time as you can on things that you love doing.** When you do this, you're more likely to become differentially better at those things than you are at others, and this distinguishes you from everyone else and creates opportunities that will light you up. Never lose sight of the things that get you excited and bring you energy.

> **Build relationships with people who lift you up and inspire you.** These relationships not only are a critical source of energy and inspiration that help you to navigate life's many challenges, but they are also almost always the source of opportunities that come your way.

> **Maintain an attitude of gratitude.** People like to be around other people who are positive, who look for the best in others, and who see opportunity where others see challenges. Regularly reflect on all the good things in your life, and appreciate how lucky you are to be alive—and share this gratitude with others.

The beauty of these three concepts in particular is that you have 100-percent control over each of them. You get to choose what you get good at. You get to choose whom you see as a role model and whom you reach out to for advice and friendship. And as things happen around you, you get to choose how you react and whether you see the glass as half full or half empty. You control all these factors 100 percent, and they're the things that will play a role every single day in shaping how your life turns out.

Sure, you'll also need to summon courage at key points in time. Being financially prudent will improve your ability to step into opportunities as they arrive—and spending your 168 hours each week in thoughtful ways is also important—but these three points reign supreme in terms of their impact on your ability to live the most inspired and fulfilling life possible. Be sure to keep these goals front and center at all times.

In the end, this book is about helping you find and follow your true north so that you can lead your best life. So many people today are living someone else's view of what their life should be and are finding themselves adrift in the sea of life, uncertain and unhappy about the path in front of them.

I hope that I have helped you break free from other people's narratives about what success looks like so that you can identify what truly inspires you as a unique individual. By enacting positive change in your daily life, setting the right goals, taking steps consistent with those goals, and overcoming the fear of the unknown, you can pivot to compelling new experiences that light you up. It's never too late to course correct and establish a new true-north plan that will make you happier and more fulfilled. This is your life, and you are the only person who knows how you can make the most of it. You have the power to turn your dreams into your destiny. The time to get started is now!

Acknowledgements

Writing a book is much more difficult than I'd imagined, but also far more rewarding. For supporting my many statements to anyone who would listen that "I'm writing a book" and for quietly going along with this notion, even knowing that I hadn't written a single sentence in years, I'd like to start by thanking my wife, Lisa. Her supportive acknowledgement of my book-writing intentions, and her willingness to serve as a sounding board while I worked to hone my views over many years, can't be understated in terms of her role in ultimately turning my book-writing fantasy into reality.

I'd also like to acknowledge my son Chris and daughter Lauren and their critical contributions to this book. Unbeknownst to either of them, they've been participating in my personal "clinical trial" for the past two-plus decades as my views on living an inspired and fulfilling life began to take shape. As I identified insights around the things most critical to living an amazing life, I would quickly work to apply these ideas to both my children, actively seeking to see what topics lit them up and supporting them in pursuing any avenues that gave them energy and naturally drew them into wanting to become better at something—not because Lisa and I said they had to, but because they innately were interested in a certain topic. Lisa and I also worked hard to help them identify role models, learn to maintain financial flexibility, learn to take risks and not overreact when things don't go exactly as they'd hoped, and all the other key principles in this book. These skills have served them well to date. They will undoubtedly remain a key part of my giant experiment for decades to come—and so far, all the signs from this experiment appear to be working out great!

Aviation has played such an important role in my life and my career journey that I'd be remiss if I didn't call out a small number of individuals who played a disproportionate role in my life achievements. Bill Copeland was a fellow in a field many years ago, flying a model airplane with his nephew, who took notice of 12-year-old me in the distance watching him with enthusiasm. He invited me over to see his model plane, and that initial encounter soon morphed into building model airplanes at his house every day after school and him picking me up every Saturday morning at 6:30 to go fly them at a local field. His mentorship and enormous time investment kindled my love of aviation and showed me how big a difference a single person can make in someone's life.

Al Knabe and Bob Oliver are two amazing aerobatic pilots from the Livermore Airport who took notice of my regular visits there as a teenager and agreed to provide me with lessons for free in exchange for my commitment to learning and helping them and others at the airport clean and maintain their planes. This was a lopsided trade with me getting far more in return than they ever received, and I owe a huge portion of my flying skills to these two individuals who went above and beyond in their time investment and mentorship to help me learn to fly with a level of skill and competence that is not accessible to the vast majority of new aviation students.

Doug Reynolds was a young flight instructor at the Livermore Airport who also noticed me, as a young kid, hanging out around the hangars and reached out to invite me along as an observer on many of his flight lessons; he then, later in his career, went out of his way to offer me copilot opportunities on some of the larger aircraft he was flying. Doug's friendship and commitment to my learning were instrumental in setting me up for the aviation adventures that would come my way over the decades that followed.

Dan Daily played a key role in both my transition to flying private jets and my introduction to the world of business. Dan was supportive of me as a new pilot joining the company he flew for, despite me being only 25 years old. Dan and I flew together for several years out of Santa Barbara, traveling all over the U.S. and the Caribbean, and this time together gave us lots of opportunities to talk about life, careers, relationships, and more. His humbleness, coaching, and guidance played a pivotal role in shaping my decisions to round out my skills beyond flying to give myself the greatest number of career and life options over the coming years.

Elwood Schapansky unknowingly had a tremendous and positive impact on my life when he gave a riveting talk at the University of California, Santa Barbara, in 1987 about his adventures as a physics professor during the school year and an Alaska bush pilot in the summer. He showcased his amazing life of adventure and lit a fire in me that I couldn't put out. His stories were an inspiration to me when, just a few months after hearing him speak, I took a leave of absence from engineering graduate school to pursue the adventures of flying in Alaska. I followed in Elwood's footsteps and headed to the Far North, where the adventures I'd dreamed of emerged, just as I'd hoped for, and set the stage for so many of my future life opportunities. Elwood and I became great friends years after he first inspired me, and to this day, his curiosity and zest for living a life well lived serve as a shining example of what's possible when one pursues one's life guided by those things that light them up.

My college years were heavily and positively influenced by two individuals in particular, namely Roger Freedman and Eric Mokover. Roger was my undergraduate physics professor (apparently, I'm drawn to individuals in this profession), and he was the most entertaining—and intelligent—of any professor I ever had. He made learning fun and intuitive, and the fact that he used so many aviation examples only served to make me like his classes that much more. We became great friends as, even as a freshman and sophomore in college, I was ahead of him in the flying journey and he was largely just starting out. I was able to impart flying wisdom on him while, at the same time, Roger was far more knowledgeable about physics and was able to impart his wisdom on me. We helped each other out and became such good friends in the process that Lisa and I eventually asked Roger to be the minister who would marry us more than a decade later. His way of teaching helped me to learn in ways others never could, and his willingness to vouch for me in scholarship and graduate-school applications undoubtedly helped me land opportunities that otherwise would have been out of my reach.

Eric Mokover played a similarly influential role for me in graduate school at UCLA. He was part of the selection committee that picked my classmate Johnna Capitano and me to colead first-year orientation. That opportunity allowed me to get to know all the UCLA MBA faculty quite well and for them to get to know me. During job interviews in the fall of my second and final year of my MBA, it was Eric's recommendation that a senior recruiter from Arthur D. Little have lunch with me just to get to know me. That same evening after having lunch with the ADL recruiter, I received an offer to join the firm as a new consultant, which then, three years later, opened the door for me to join McKinsey & Company, which then opened so many other doors. I'm enormously thankful for both Roger's and Eric's contributions during my university years and for the opportunities that came my way directly as a result of their investments in my life.

My professional working years after college were shaped by so many incredible people, though there are a few who absolutely had outsized impact on my path in life and the opportunities that came my way. Endre Holen was a senior partner at McKinsey who took me under his wing early in my consulting career and invested countless hours in coaching to help me learn to be an effective client leader. Endre is one of the best problem solvers and client advisors I've ever worked with, and his commitment over more than 10 years to my development had a profound impact on my success and the opportunities that came my way. We developed a symbiotic relationship in which I was able to impart my love of aviation, which opened up a whole new life for him as an accomplished professional pilot after retiring from McKinsey, while he imparted on me a set of skills that serve me well every day in the corporate world. It was his personal recommendation several years ago that resulted in me getting the amazing role I stepped into at Cisco. Endre continues to coach me and challenge me to be the best I can be, and we remain great flying buddies who share a common love of aviation.

Marc Singer played an equally profound role in my success as a leader. Marc is the McKinsey partner who took the chance on me and made me the offer to join the company back in 1998. I didn't match the typical profile of a McKinsey consultant, but Marc saw something in me that I hadn't yet seen. Marc coached me as I ramped up in the intense world of management consulting and showed me a style of leadership that resonated deeply with me. Marc's approach to people development and client leadership was always thoughtful, without politics or drama, and highly considered. I saw in Marc a style of leadership that felt very genuine and aligned with my own "style," and that gave me hope that although my approach to life was different than that of many of my McKinsey colleagues, I could craft a path that would allow me to be successful in the consulting world while also staying true to the other things that matter deeply to me. Marc had the perfect mix of attributes that elevated him to role-model status—and he continues to serve as an inspiration to this day.

I'd also like to acknowledge two individuals who played a surprisingly important role in my life journey despite having little to no direct interactions with me: Sir Richard Branson and Bob Hoover. As I talk about in this book, role models are critically important to shaping life goals and for gaining the confidence that there's a path in front of you that might actually be achievable. Richard's story of building the Virgin empire is so inspiring, and the fact that he was able to do what he did while not taking himself too seriously was hugely inspiring to me and helped shape a lot of my own views on leadership. Similarly, Bob Hoover had some of the most inspiring flying and leadership stories throughout his career, and despite how accomplished he became, he always remained one of the most approachable and kind people I've ever met. He even sent me a personal voicemail years ago after hearing that I'd volunteered to pick him up to fly him to a Hall of Fame award ceremony. He ended up getting a ride from someone else, and he didn't have to call me, but he did call to say "thank you"—and that just showed the depth of his character and that he was appreciative of all that came to him, regardless of how much he had already achieved in his life. His approach to life and adventure has influenced me greatly.

I'd be remiss if I didn't acknowledge the huge contributions of Amelia Forczak. She and her team at Pithy Wordsmithery were the "secret ingredient" to me finally turning my two-decade intention of writing a book into something real. Amelia's knowledge and expertise of the complex book-writing journey has been invaluable, and her ability to push my thinking to get the fullness of my perspectives down in writing meant far more than I had expected. Although the perspectives in this book are fully mine, for sure they would not be as complete were it not for Amelia.

And last, but certainly not least, I'd like to thank my mom and dad, Patricia and Lyn Pleasance. They were both perceptive and courageous enough to see my innate love of aviation during my teenage years and leaned in to support me in ways that many other parents would not have. Their support was not so much financial but rather was something far more powerful and impactful: they gave me encouragement, and they listened to the things that mattered most to me. They said yes when I was offered my first airplane ride from a gentleman at the airport; they said yes when supporting me in prioritizing a university that was close to an airport so I could keep flying while I went to college; and they said yes to so many other things I got excited about and wanted to dig deeper into to learn more. They didn't impose their views on what was "best for me" other than helping me to navigate the various paths that lit me up and occupied so many of my thoughts and dreams over so many years. For this gift, I owe no one a greater expression of gratitude than I do my parents.

There were countless others who played an outsized role in my life journey—far too many to mention here. However, I must acknowledge a few of them who contributed disproportionately in recent years: Francoise Brougher, Cyndi and Alden DeSoto, Gerri Elliott, Michael Goulian, Tim and Karen Hensley, Megan Karnopp, Chris Luvara, Maria Martinez, Tom Poberezny, Cyrus Sigari, Erik Stephansen, Jim Thomas, Alan Thygesen, and Will Warne. Each of them has made a substantial contribution to my life and my accomplishments, and for this I am eternally grateful.

About Darren Pleasance

Darren truly embodies the expression of living life to the fullest. Over his four-decade-long career, Darren has worked for some of the most influential and admired companies in the world, including Google, Cisco, and McKinsey & Company, while also rising to the top echelons of the aviation world as a corporate jet pilot, aerobatic competitor, Alaska bush pilot, vintage warbird pilot, and flight instructor.

Darren is also an "extreme" do-it-yourselfer, utilizing the power of the internet to learn how to do virtually anything, from running large earth-moving equipment to overhauling gasoline engines to fixing appliances and more. Darren loves to learn and finds ways to preserve this interest all while growing and succeeding in the fast-paced world of corporate America.

Darren currently lives in Bend, a quaint ski town in Central Oregon. He and his wife Lisa elected to move there in 2006 to embrace the zest for adventure they both craved while also creating a great environment for raising both of their kids. Darren has been able to preserve his love of flying by piloting his plane regularly to and from his company's headquarters in the San Francisco Bay Area.

Darren's life journey has afforded him the opportunity to work with a wide spectrum of inspiring and influential people, from astronauts to movie stars to business owners to politicians as well as "regular" people who struggle with all the same challenges that other "mere mortals" do. It has been through this journey, and from these relationships, that Darren has stitched together his views, and the views of others, on those elements that are most important for living an inspired life. He loves exploring what it means to find personal fulfillment, breaking free from others' expectations, and how to know when we have "enough."

Darren is a frequent speaker on living an inspiring life as well as a variety of topics in the aviation and technology sectors. He is passionate about technology trends and the influence these trends have on the world.

Endnotes

1. Interview with Dr. Colleen Cira, June 5, 2023.

2. James Clear, *Atomic Habits* (Penguin Random House, 2018).

3. K. Anders Ericsson, Ralf Th. Krampe, and Clemens Tesch-Romer, "The Role of Deliberate Practice in the Acquisition of Expert Performance," *Psychological Review*, vol. 100, no. 3 (1993): 363–406.

4. Interview with Deke Sharron, April 2023.

5. Obituary/poem, *The New Yorker*, May 2005.

6. Eric Mack, "The Exact Amount of Money It Takes to Make a Person Happy Just Got an Update," Inc.com, https://www.inc.com/eric-mack/the-exact-amount-of-money-it-takes-to-make-a-person-happy-just-got-an-update.html (accessed Oct. 16, 2023).

7. Jacqueline DeMarco, "Average US Salary by State," SoFi.com, https://www.sofi.com/learn/content/average-salary-in-us/#:~:text=The%20average%20annual%20average%20salary,by%20outlying%20numbers%2C%20is%20%2456%2C420 (accessed Oct. 16, 2023).

8. "Taking Control: Financial Strategies for Women," Country Financial, 2022.

9. Peter F. Drucker *The Practice of Management* (Harper Business; Reissue edition 2010).

10. Francesca Gino et al., "Reclaim Your Commute," *Harvard Business Review*, May–June 2017, https://hbr.org/2017/05/reclaim-your-commute (accessed Oct. 16, 2023).

11. Tanza Loudenback, "Study: Adding 20 Minutes to Your Commute Makes You as Miserable as Getting a 19 Percent Pay Cut," Business Insider, https://www.inc.com/business-insider/study-reveals-commute-time-impacts-job-satisfaction.html (accessed Oct. 16, 2023).

12. Interview with Dr. Colleen Cira, June 5, 2023.

13. Rick Werry, *Red Letter Days* (Rick Werry, 2022).

14. Kathleen J. Sullivan, "Transfer student is forging a new life path at Stanford," Stanford Report, Feb. 4, 2021, https://news.stanford.edu/report/2021/02/04/transfer-student-forging-new-life-path-stanford/.

15. "Jason Spyres," ASU + GSV Summit, https://www.asugsvsummit.com/speakers/jason-spyres (accessed Aug. 15, 2023).

16. "North American P-51 Mustang," Wikipedia, https://en.wikipedia.org/wiki/North_American_P-51_Mustang (accessed Oct. 16, 2023).

Appendix

DEFINING AN INSPIRED LIFE

What matters to you?	Score (H, M, L)	Notes
Pursuing passions		
Mastery		
Meaningful connections/ relationships		
Being around other people		
Purpose		
Home		
Physical belongings		
Amount of free time		
Autonomy		
Location		
Hobbies/activities that bring you joy		
Personal growth		
Spirituality		
Exercise		
Travel		
Adventure		
Stability		
Community Service		

- Score each dimension as High, Medium, or Low.
- Limit yourself to no more than 5 "High's"
- Make notes on why those are "high"; also make notes on why you called anything out as "low"; this will help you get grounded in what matters most and least to you

EXERCISE 2: **CREATE A ROADMAP**

Key Questions	Notes

What is a long-term outcome you want to achieve?

Why to you want to achieve that outcome?

What are the emotions you associate with that outcome?

What are some short term outcomes that would help you make progress toward achieving the long-term outcome?

What are actions you will need to take to achieve both short- and long-term outcomes?

- Use this worksheet for as many long-term outcomes as you'd like to set for yourself
- For each one, work through the questions to arrive at the tangible actions you could commit yourself to taking that would systematically move you closer to those outcomes over time
- Keep these actions visible to yourself as a reminder on a regular basis of what you need to be doing to achieve the outcome(s) you're wanting
- Be honest with yourself; if you're not taking the required actions, or are taking actions inconsistent with the outcome you want, ask yourself "why" and enlist friends or mentors to hold you accountable: Say what you'll do, and do what you say

EXERCISE 3: **YOUR TOP 5**

5 People you Spend the Most Time With	Their overall effect on you (better, neutral, worse)	Notes

- What qualities and characteristics do they possess?
- How do they generally affect your mindset, attitude, and overall mood?
- Do they support your personal growth and goals? If so, how?
- Are their values and beliefs aligned with yours? If not, in what ways do they differ?
- Are they individuals who help you be a better you (learn new skills, meet inspiring people, push past your natural insecurities)?

People who make you Better	Opportunities to spend MORE time with them?

People who make you Worse	Opportunities to LIMIT / ELIMINATE time with them?

New people you'd like in your life	Ideas for connecting with these individuals: Friends, LinkedIn, Conferences, Join Same Group, Blind Outreach, ...

DARREN PLEASANCE

EXERCISE 4: WHAT LIGHTS YOU UP?

Key Questions	Notes

What do you want to be known for?

What experiences would you love to have be part of your story when you're looking back on your life many years from now?

What changes would you like to affect in the world if you could?

Who are the types of people you most admire and what is it about them that you admire?

What paths in life did you not take because someone earlier in your life said no or talked you out of it?

How do you choose to spend your free time, and where do you naturally procrastinate? (What magazines do you pick up when you have a free moment? What YouTube videos do you find yourself wanting to watch the most? Who are the people you like to read about or listen to? What is it about them that intrigues you?)

DARREN PLEASANCE

EXERCISE 5: **YOUR IDEAL 168 HOURS?**

100% = 168 Hours

				Meditating (XX)	
Wellness (XX)	Sleep (XX)		Eating (XX)		Exercising (XX)
Career (XX)	Focus 1 (XX) Focus 2 (XX)		Focus 3 (XX)		Focus 4 (XX) Focus 5 (XX)
Chores (XX)	Finances (XX)		Housework (XX)		Errands (XX)
Relationships (XX)	Spouse (XX)		Kids (XX)	Relatives (XX)	Friends (XX)
Me Time (XX)	Energizer 1 (XX)		Energizer 2 (XX)		Energizer 3 (XX)

Made in the USA
Monee, IL
16 December 2023

49515725R00121